CONTENT WARFARE

HOW TO FIND YOUR AUDIENCE,
TELL YOUR STORY
AND WIN THE BATTLE
FOR ATTENTION ONLINE

RYAN HANLEY

Volume orders available upon request. Email ryan@ryanhanley.com for details.

...to my wife.

When I was lost in a sea of complacency,

you saw potential and pulled me ashore.

Contents

V

« Acknowledgements »

This book exists because of 142 people, the contributors to the crowdfunding campaign which validated the concept behind Content Warfare and financed its production.

The trust and faith you placed in me by pledging hard-earned money towards a project that did not yet exist was the rocket fuel propelling every keystroke.

Thank you...

Josh Cary, Jill Roth, Kristina Preisner, Melissa Murphy, Carlos Vargas, Jason Cass, Jeff Roy, Josh Richner, Charles Payet, Eric Borgeson, Claudia McClain, Gina Fiedel, Guy Vincent, Jay Baer, Jeremy Abel, Matthew Rouse, Natalie Sisson, Pat Alexander, Mark Sheldon, Robbie MacCue, Todd Smith, Tommy Walker, Tracey Canfield, Chris Langille, Denny Christner, Samantha Ashdown, Alan Quarry, Tina Thor Jorgensen, Will Muroe, Bronwyn White, Carol Lynn Rivera, Eric Wagner, John Parsons, Matthew Davison, Jason Mulholland, Steve Brodie, Richard Hauswirth, Adrian de Canha, Amelia Hoskins, Ann-Marie Eu, Arn Betteridge, Chef Dennis Littley, Scott Harrigan, Agnes Knowles, Bob Strassel Jr, Brent Kelly, Brett Cohrs, Bill Richards, Bryan Caporicci, Christine DeGraff, Dawn Augustine, Dave Berndt, David Gerbino, Deborah Tutnauer, Didier Daglinckx, Don Stanley, Dan Sage, Edward Baker, Carol Clokey, Emily Huling, Felicia Rateliff, Bruce Brodeen, Dedek Hajes, Carrie Reynolds, Jahnan Derso, Courtney Sullivan, Jacob Lerner, Jason Pedwell, Jan Beckman, Joey Morkes, Joey Giangola, John Murphy, Joshua Lipstone, Jan Koch, Krithika Rangarajan, Keith Laskey, Lisa McGuire, Luca De Berardinis, Maris Munkevics, Martin Shervington, Marylyn Broomhall, Matthew Byers, Michelle Aguilar, Eric Narcisco, Paul Rhynard, Tim O'Brien, Fabio Ramos, Robert Baggett, Robin Roelofsen, Roger Edwards, Samuel Knowles, Stephan Hovnanian, ST Billingsley, S Loschiavo, Tim Dodge, Tim Danyo, Tim Bain, Tom Morkes, Wade Harman, Wendy Hernandez, Andre Fernandes, Anna Caban, Barry Tan, Carolyn Capern, Chip Thompson, Chris Gaffney, Christian Karasiewicz, Chris Leonard, Larry Taylor, Dale Bateman, Dan Dynneson, Dave Willis, Denise Wakeman, Lisa Saline, Duke Revard, Ed Sward, Heather Ratcliff, Iris Van Kerckhove, James Dearsley, Jason Hoeppner, Jeff Sieh, Jason Frasca, Looi Qin En, Lisa Engles, Larry Michael,

Lyn Bowker, Marc DeLeonibus, Mary Stovall, Narelle Redman, Rick Morgan, Roy Blumenthal, Sandra Masters, Simon Payn, Jeff Korhan, Jerome Syed, Mia Voss, and last but most certainly not least Mark Traphagen.

Special Acknowledgement

I'd also like to give special acknowledgement to a few people who without their support, guidance and expertise this project would have never reached escape velocity.

To my wife Lauren, for all the reasons only you and I will ever know, thank you.

To my son Duke: you are my rocket fuel.

Thank you to Tom Morkes, who made the introduction, that turned someday into today.

Thank you to Guy Vincent, mission control of my crowdfunding voyage.

Thank you to Tom Owens and his talented wife Diana Helmer for understanding my vision for this book and helping turn a meandering series of words into a meaningful story.

Thank you to Craig McBreen, for embodying Content Warfare in his work, and for writing a fantastic foreword to this book.

Thank you to Mars Dorian, for sticking with me and not holding back on the amazing cover design for this book.

Thank you to Jason Cass, whose friendship means more to me than I'll be able to express, and for pushing me to be more than I was yesterday.

Thank you to Marcus Sheridan: In the times I've needed guidance the most, you've been the friend and mentor I needed, whether you realize it or not.

Lastly, an extra special thank you goes to all the **Content Warriors** who read the blog, engage on social media, attend my presentations and listen to the podcast... it's always been about you. You honor me every day with your presence, a fact I will never forget.

« Preface »

"Better a diamond with a flaw than a pebble without." ~ Confucius

As of the final draft of this book, I've been a Dad for nine months. An incomparable, indescribable human experience. I do not possess the poetic gift to adequately paint a picture of the moment Duke was placed in my arms.

If you're a parent, you know.

Excitement. Terror. Joy. Anxiety. Love. More love than I had previously believed possible. Intense, diametrically opposed forces pulling on my soul. As every expectant parent hears a thousand and one times, I knew my life would never be the same. But not because I had this new, very time-consuming Obligation relying upon me and my wife for survival.

No, not an obligation. Nothing so shallow or selfish.

The moment he was placed in my arms, I was given purpose. In a breath, every priority in my life changed. This was MY son. A piece of my soul had been peeled away to create him.

My purpose, my responsibility, was to help him become the best version of himself. Tap into whatever potential he may be blessed with.

And here he sits, right next to me, cooing as he dreams his baby dreams and I share my thoughts with you. *What life will he live?*

Then it hits me: I can only teach him what I live myself. I want him to know possibility. I want him to know creativity. I want him to believe in a world beyond what we see today. He will be my greatest creative endeavor.

In order to help him, I must first live the creative life I've repressed for so long. I must see the world as I hope my son will see it, because I've lived in cubicle hell. I've been the cog in the machine. Worse, I thought my job on the 23rd floor of 3 World Financial Center in Downtown Manhattan was success, in and of itself.

For all intents and purposes, I was stamping reports, like Peter Gibbons in *Office Space*. I had three bosses within eyesight of my desk and, just like *Office Space*, they regularly stopped by my *"Work space"* to check in on my *"Progress."*

The truth is, just like me, they were bored. Except none of us had the balls to admit it. Every day, I felt more useless, helpless and dull. Conversations with co-workers focused more on which sandwich we'd choose from the company cafeteria than the work sitting on our desks. When lunch was over, all we talked about was leaving.

The corporate cog is a life I wouldn't wish upon my worst enemy.

I felt uncreative, uninspired and underwhelmed by the life I was living and the contribution I was making to it. Inside us all is an intrinsic desire to provide value to the community we live in.

The Internet has made the concept of "Community" very broad but, whatever community you live in, it is your obligation to feed it with creative energy. *Most people don't. Most won't. Most can't.*

Not because they're incapable, but rather because they've never opened their eyes to creativity. Life changes when we make ourselves available to creativity.

I learned this at 30 years old.

Creativity wasn't frowned upon in my household growing up . . . but it wasn't encouraged, either. My parents viewed creativity as a luxury of people who didn't worry about bills (because those people were either so rich or so poor).

Can you imagine growing up thinking of creativity as a luxury? I repressed my own creativity because I'd never been rich, and didn't want to be poor. So I did what I thought we're supposed to do: nuzzle up to the corporate teat.

It's sad to think about today. But a sadder scenario would be to perpetuate the cycle with my son. He doesn't have to choose a creative life, but his creativity will be given respect. His creativity will be cultivated and encouraged. And, with a little bit of luck, he'll marry his creative passion with a satisfying career.

The new American Dream: **The creative-preneur.** A man tuned into his own creativity. It's my job to hold the platform higher for my son than it was held for me.

This book is his first breadcrumb.

In the small, upstate New York town I grew up in, Thursday was recycling day. Every Wednesday night the town folk would collect all their bottles and cans from around the house to put on the curb in blue recycling bins, to be picked up the next morning. Dirty and cracked by years of abuse from weather and indifferent garbage collectors, the blue bins were, to most people, nothing more than an eyesore in our quaint town.

Yet to me, a boy of humble beginnings, never without necessities but often without luxuries, those blue bins represented opportunity.

Every Thursday I'd wake up at four thirty in the morning, get dressed, and head out with a pocket full of garbage bags. My town was thirty minutes from the nearest grocery store, and most people were too lazy to make the half-hour drive to return their bottles and cans for the five-cent deposit.

Our brains work differently as children. We don't consider what other people think. We know what we don't like, and we think of ways to fix those things without regard to outside judgment, criticism or questioning.

In my child brain, every bottle and can was a little piece of opportunity. Opportunity to NOT be the poor kid in the neighborhood. We forget, as adults, that opportunities are made of our own doing; opportunities are never *given*.

As a small-town 10-year old, I saw LOTS of opportunity in a couple of extra dollars.

I saw myself as industrious and entrepreneurial. The disapproving looks

I received through the blinds of my neighbors' windows told a different story. But at age ten, I didn't care. I saw opportunity at the bottom of every dirty, sticky, broken blue plastic bin.

As the weeks passed, I began to see patterns. I knew who the drinkers were; I knew who put their cans and bottles back in the cartons. This made my stops at certain houses much quicker. I started to ride my bike through the neighborhoods after school just to plot out my course, so I could cover more ground on Recycling Day.

On a good day, I might collect three to four garbage bags full of bottles. Dragging the full plastic bags behind took too much time, so I paid a friend a dollar for his old toy wagon, and collection numbers went even higher. At the height of my bottle collecting career, I was making twenty dollars a week. At five cents a bottle, that's 400 bottles a morning.

These days, a ten-year-old with twenty dollars in his pocket isn't that impressive. But in 1991, in my small town, I was rich. Do you think my friends made fun of my career when I was buying them all bubble gum and baseball cards? Heck, no.

A couple of them even offered to go into business with me and, for a few months in the spring of 1991, I franchised my bottle collection business into a couple of neighborhoods I didn't have time to reach on my own.

I saw opportunity at the bottom of a blue recycling bin, and what started as a way to make some pocket money turned into a business.

After eight months of fat pockets and growing revenues, my neighbors began to catch on to what I was doing. Blue bins in front of houses I used to bank on for large stashes of bottles began to turn up empty and, just like that, my first career was coming to an end. It didn't help that I had competition as well: an adult in town figured out my game, and began collecting bottles himself. He had a car.

Here's the scoop on opportunity:

Opportunities are made, not given . . . and often beget more opportunity.

By this time, I had gotten a taste of success, and had already started another business. I had bought so many baseball cards with my bottle earnings that I began hustling them to friends and schoolmates for a profit.

If I had been self-conscious, I wouldn't have been a kid walking cold streets at four thirty in the morning collecting garbage. I would have allowed public perception to stop me from creating income where it hadn't been before. How many future opportunities would I have missed?

A lot, I'm going to guess.

I'm sharing this story with you because it's one of the first stories I want to share with my son when he's old enough to understand. We can't buy into this *"You only get one opportunity"* nonsense. You get as many opportunities as you make for yourself.

"Opportunity" isn't always sexy or popular. But "Success" has a way of washing clean the dirt of humble beginnings.

My son may never pick bottles from recycling bins for cash (I hope his opportunities involve fewer chances of bacterial infection!) But I know that, for an opportunity to be satisfying, he'll have to make it himself.

Don't romanticize opportunity. We can't wrap every opportunity in a nice neat bow and take it home to Mom. In my case, opportunity was waiting at the bottom of a dirty blue recycling bin. I just had to reach down inside and take it.

Take it I did, and I have no regrets, because mediocrity scares the shit out of me.

Average. Ordinary. Standard. Usual. Normal. Typical. Common. Customary. Regular. Every-day. The idea that I was conceived, built, grown and launched into this world to be nothing more than "run-of-the-mill" is simply unacceptable.

Some may see this as a silly, contrived fear. *How can someone find fear in being average?* Average is safe. That's why we all strive to achieve the same things in life: safety, security and sanctuary.

Don't second-guess the standard process. Don't question the usual path, because people who break free from mediocrity aren't normal. They're radicals, rebels, and rabble-rousers. They wipe their asses with typical.

Typical is the murderer of thought, the defiler of ideas, the jailer of genius. *Typical* is the synapse you've already burned into that genius brain of yours, and *typical* leads right to the lizard brain.

The lizard brain wants us all to be the same. A flock of geese. A herd of cattle. Middle management. The lizard brain tells us to avoid trouble. "Don't rock the boat," says the lizard brain. And we listen.

So we put in the time, we pay our dues, and we pray that, someday, everything works out. *That the cubicle will become an office. That the hourly wage will become a salary. That the job will become a career. That our sensibility will become success.*

XIV   We make the choices that lead to Mediocrity.

I fear mediocrity more than death, because one is my choice, and one is not.

We don't choose to die, but it's going to happen anyway. Why fear something you can't avoid?

I fear mediocrity more than death, because one is my choice and one is not.

Fear courses through my veins at the possibility of living a typical life. Debilitating, gut-wrenching, sweat-inducing fear.

Fear of hopes not achieved. Fear of childhood dreams cast aside for the security of a life not questioned, not critiqued. Fear of never really being alive, of never taking a risk, of never putting myself on display, naked and alone, vulnerable to inquisition.

Fear of never feeling the pain of defeat, of failure. Fear of being average. Fear of being no different than you.

I don't mean I want to be better than you; I do mean I want to be different. How can I add value to your life if our regular lives are exactly the same? *Am I supposed to help you become more typical? More mediocre? More regular?*

I've always dreamed of denting the world. Not because I have some unique gift others are incapable of providing, but because I simply have the desire.

Creation destroys mediocrity. Creation, my friend: The bright light in our would-be dark, mediocre lives. Creation is my prayer, my meditation, my salvation from leading a mediocre life.

This is the lesson I hope you take from **Content Warfare:** that to succeed (in the digital world, as in life), we must outwork our competition in creating an audience, creating a story and, ultimately, in creating the attention that fuels our business.

To harness creation at will in my business, I've allowed my creativity to flow over into every aspect of my life. One day it's singing old country songs to put my son to bed. The next it might be making my wife laugh so hard she has to pee. Tonight it's writing.

My point is this: mediocrity is a derivative of our surrender to the lizard brain. The lizard brain says: *Don't create; don't stick out; don't be different. There is no safety or security in being different. Stand out and you will be scrutinized, you will be criticized, you will experience failure and you will feel pain.*

Listen to the lizard brain and you will be safe, you will be secure . . . and you will be mediocre. But you will never experience what "completely awesome" feels like, even if only for a moment, and you will certainly never be the person you were conceived, built, grown and launched into this world to become.

Mediocrity scares the shit out of me because I am now a father, and my son will see my life as a template for his own.

In this book I will ask you to look deep inside yourself. Deeper than other content marketing "How-to" and list post blogs have ever taken you.

Prepare to redefine how brands build and extract value from their online audiences. Whether you're a solopreneur struggling to make ends meet, a salesperson trying to wear two hats, or a marketing professional inside a Fortune 500 company, a seminal understanding of how to win the battle for attention online can be yours.

Ryan Hanley

Albany, NY

« Foreword »

by Craig McBreen

In late spring, 2011, I did something out of the ordinary. For me, it was way beyond business as usual:

I resurrected my Twitter account, created a mug shot (read: avatar), and started consuming one blog after another. But the unheard-of part was that I started commenting on blogs.

It was a rebirth of sorts.

Yep. For most of my life, I was the kind of person who avoided any kind of attention. So how ironic that, almost three years later, I'm writing the foreword to a book that has "Win the Battle for Attention" in its subtitle.

I've been trying to earn online attention for three years, and during that time I've learned:

> » Working to attract eyeballs and ears is a grind, so prepare for a marathon, not a sprint.

> » t's hard to get it right the first time. In fact, I think most people stumble, see the herculean task ahead of them, get discouraged, and drop out.

Winning the battle for attention is where your intestinal fortitude will be tested. The phrase "tough work" doesn't even begin to do it justice. But there's a big, fat benefit I've not yet mentioned: embarking on this journey could change your life.

The Power of Self-Promotion

Let's be frank: if you're blogging or podcasting or shooting video (Ryan does all three), you're screaming for attention. But guess what? This is more than okay. In fact, it might be the only way to survive this new age.

According to bestselling author James Altucher, this is the "choose yourself" era, and those who learn to effectively promote themselves and their businesses will be the creative souls left standing when the smoke clears (or the robots take over).

In 2011, I kinda 'got' this. By 2014, I *completely* got it. The years between were a pick-and-shovel period for me, a back-breaking stretch full of stops and starts. I was a 40-something babe-in-the-woods figuring it out as I went, all while balancing the craziness of life.

However, I am so grateful I chose this path. I've always had a burning desire to 'break out' and, for this recovering introvert, the online world was my space to do it.

I'm not ashamed to admit that I've been working to win the battle for attention online. I believe it's changed my life for the better. I hope it does the same for you.

When you read Ryan's grounded, inspirational message, you might be sparked to start building an online presence, or to re-map your current path—but your journey won't be filled with false starts. That's because his message is infused with truth, versus phooey hinting you can run your

business while sipping margaritas on some tropical beach.

Ryan is all about building a powerful yet sustainable online presence, filled to the brim with value. His is a viable yet robust model where you find your tribe, give them what they need, and grow a community built on creativity, honesty and sweat equity.

But before you read his wise words, consider reading mine, where I do my best to frame Ryan's content. Because to me this book is about . . .

1. *Truth.* Or to be more specific, fighting the myth of "overnight success."

2. *Creativity.* A huge part of online success comes when you rediscover your innovative spirit.

3. *Balance.* Where combining wicked business sense with your playful side can lead to magic.

→ **So, let's go . . .**

1. Truth

Let's clear the air.

Before you try and earn attention, you must let something go.

In case you haven't noticed, the dropout rate in the blogosphere is staggering, and one of the main reasons for this is a myth that is propagated far and wide.

I would go so far as to call this deception an online disease, because tail-wagging beginners see those rare "skyrocketing" success stories and think a formula is there for the taking.

They're "infected" with the myth of "Overnight Success." And some of the most prolific blog authors out there are gifted at spreading this viral message.

To date, the best quote I've read on this topic comes from the book "Rework" by Jason Fried:

The myth of the overnight sensation

You will not be a big hit right away. You will not get rich quick. You are not so special that everyone else will instantly pay attention. No one cares about you. At least not yet. Get used to it.

You know those overnight-success stories you've heard about? It's not the whole story. Dig deeper and you'll usually find people who have busted their asses for years to get into a position where things could take off. And on the rare occasion that instant success does come along, it usually doesn't last—there's no foundation there to support it.

Trade the dream of overnight success for slow, measured growth. It's hard, but you have to be patient. You have to grind it out. You have to do it for a long time before the right people notice.

And, as Ryan states in this book, " . . . attention is fleeting in nature and discriminating in quality."

So true.

The words you are about to read are all about getting attention, yes. But Mr. Hanley has no snake oil to sell. He's an honest guy with humble roots, who's been in the trenches and knows the blood, sweat and tears it takes to earn attention and keep it.

And I'm certain he'd be the first to tell you that overnight success is a sham, built for weak minds and engineered for quick sales.

Now, if you're the sort who is open to slow, incremental progress (baby steps) versus the dream of becoming an overnight sensation (utter rubbish), I think you're in the right place.

2. Creativity

When writing about his new son, Duke, Ryan states, "To help him, I must first live the creative life I've repressed for so long."

This made me think back to when my first son was born. He reignited a fire that had been repressed for a long time. When he came into the world, he sparked me to action.

Soon after my son was born, I started my own business—and something I'll call "creative spirit" was a huge part of that change.

Ryan is quite a bit younger than I am, but I feel we are on similar trajectories in the online world. I also think we are kindred spirits. We've both worked in corporate America, but we detest the daily slog with its backdrop of gray fabric walls, industrial carpet, and a cog-like feeling that's the ultimate spirit-crusher.

The worst part is the din of background noise, the sound of your creative soul slowly being sucked from your body. But it is a mollifying noise that lures you into submission, and gently sucks the life blood—your creative spirit— right out of you with soft, gentle whispers bathed in gray.

It makes you feel as if you're in a box with no escape.

Do you hear it?

Well, guess what? There is an escape, if escape is what you're looking for.

A huge part of this is simply falling back in love with your creative side, and working to silence that soft yet soul-crushing noise.

Creativity. You know, that other "you" last seen in elementary school?

If you're creating any form of content online, it's easy to fall into the trap of best practices, buzz-speak, and writing like a salesman (vs. teacher). If you do this, you will soon realize you've created a self-imposed prison, not too unlike your former job. You find yourself generating boring, lifeless material that does nothing for that artist within.

Content Marketing doesn't have to be like this.

What can it be? **Content Marketing** can be a practice that grows your business, but also nourishes your creative soul, freeing you to explore and think more in terms of adventure. That fire inside you that's been repressed for so damn long becomes the spark to invigorate your community

And you.

Just learn to get creative again. This will open up a whole new world, and you'll never look back.

3. Balance

So, I've been The Nagging Parent, instructing you to forget about overnight fame, which sounds rather, well … parental.

Then I became The Flighty Creative, telling you to reignite your creative side, which might sound a bit too precious and dreamy.

Well, guess what? The two don't have to be mutually exclusive.

And I am *not* telling you to forget about shooting for the stars. In fact, I'm simply showing you the hybrid model of the modern entrepreneur.

The "choose yourself" model mentioned earlier.

Ryan doesn't place every "opportunity" in a sexy cloak. He tells it like it is. But he also encourages you to aim high, dream big and push your boundaries. And that's where this book becomes part art and part science, and why I'm completely on board with his message.

Ryan doesn't like boilerplate. I bet you don't like it, either.

At the same time, he doesn't feed you "blogging on the beach" pablum for easy consumption.

In Ryan's world, run-of-the-mill is unacceptable, but so are the unrealistic promises peddled by so many.

In "Content Warfare," Ryan provides a hard dose of reality (read: pragmatism) that a small business owner like me loves. Even so, his core message is sparked by innate creativity, and powered by a contagious enthusiasm.

Yes, you need business sensibility, but you also must kiss your creative side, and embrace fear daily. That's the nut you must crack.

Art, science, and a little of your own magic. This is how to find your audience, tell your story and win the battle for attention.

Enjoy.

Craig McBreen

Seattle, WA

Why Content Warfare?

This book assumes that you want more out of your content marketing.

There is advice contained within this book that will make you uncomfortable. I'm going to ask you to look deep inside, both yourself and the work you're doing, and question your current content marketing activities.

My only request is that you're honest with yourself while reading this book. Comfort was not my goal while putting this work together.

Should comfort ever be a goal? No. Comfort is the last step before your work starts to die.

Comfort is a terrible goal. Striving for comfort is like drinking newly expired milk. It's not going to kill you, but you certainly aren't going to feel good about yourself in a few hours.

So if you're looking for content marketing tactics or strategies that are "Set it and forget it," you've purchased the wrong book.

I'm sorry. Please pass it along to someone else.

Freedom, wealth, time, fame, respect . . . all great goals. Not all necessarily conducive to stable emotional states, but great goals. I think about what I was like when I used to work for American Express in New York City.

I had a comfortable salary. I sat in a comfortable chair. I had a comfortable apartment. I had a comfortable life.

This was the job that College had prepared me for: at a well-respected public company in the financial district of the greatest city on earth.

But I was miserable.

Mind you, this feeling had nothing to do with American Express. I was 26 years old and completely comfortable.

But my brain was *off*. I was sleepwalking through life.

I lasted nine months in that job and quit. I quit the highest paying job I'd ever had, working for one of the most respected financial institutions in the world, in the greatest city in the world, because I couldn't live with my brain turned off.

I vowed to never live that way again. I cannot advocate work which supports you living with your brain turned off either. Our brains need challenge or they dull.

So sure, I could fill this book with article-spinning and funnel-filling strategies that allow you to kick your feet up and make some money today. But what happens when things change?

What happens when Google suddenly takes Authorship away, like they did in August of 2014?

How do you adjust? Do you go buy another book, and try to copy *that* author's strategies?

Screw that. This isn't *that* book. I'm not that guy and, as a Content Warrior, you aren't either. I wouldn't wish comfort on my worst enemy. No one deserves the malaise of comfort.

No more sleepwalking. No more "Set it and Forget it." Time to wake up and get to work.

Content Warfare is a content marketing anthem to the foundational strategies of long-term success online. It's a battle plan for growing your audience, to grow your business. The concepts and strategies you're about to learn will demand you take action (*or hire someone to take action for you*). So get your yellow highlighter, sticky notepad, or finger (if you're reading on an eReader) ready.

Let's get to work.

» We All Must Cut Our Teeth

Your industry is not unique. There are no external forces keeping you from successfully building an audience online, and ultimately extracting value in the form of brand reach, customer loyalty and revenue.

How do I know this? Because much of this book is my own experience. To help you understand my confidence in content marketing, it will help to know where I cut my teeth in content marketing.

» The Setup

My digital marketing career started in a 40-year-old independent insurance agency in upstate New York. It will help you to know that, across the country, independent insurance agents stand shoulder-to-shoulder with any other business owners in their reluctance to adopt even basic digital marketing principles (although, by 2014, change was slowly coming).

Starting sometime in 2002, my agency had a brochure-style website with four web pages. If you had checked the site in March of 2011, you'd have found it hadn't been updated since sometime in 2008. The truth is, the business had never really needed a website. The agency owner (who is also my father-in-law) had done an amazing job of building a network of referral sources inside his client base. That made the idea of spending time, money and resources on the Internet seem silly.

But as a young insurance producer (age 26), without the luxury of experience or long-term contacts, I quickly became acutely aware of how hard selling insurance can be.

People simply did not take me seriously. It didn't help that, in general, I have a young look, so at 26 I looked maybe 18. Convince business owners to put the fates of their businesses in 26-year-old hands? I might as well have asked to take their daughters on my motorcycle. No trust.

Then one day, I attended a local chamber of commerce networking event. As with almost every event I attended, I spent most of my time elbowing my way into the little circles that formed throughout the room (think high school dance, only with adults in formal business attire). On this particular day, I'd finally made my way into such a circle, only to watch the people I'd wanted to speak to begin to leave (in this case, a Real Estate Agent and a Mortgage Broker. Both were promising referral sources for an independent insurance agent).

As they were leaving, the Real Estate Agent said something to the Mortgage Broker that changed the course of my life: "Let's just connect on LinkedIn."

This was 2009. I had no clue what LinkedIn was. I had *heard* of it (maybe). The name sounded familiar, but I had no idea what was going on there.

Then the light bulb went off. In that moment a paradigm shifted in my mind, and set me on the course I'm navigating today.

There were conversations happening online I was not a part of. There were conversations that could help me grow my business, that I could not take part in, because I wasn't there.

Mind blown.

I immediately left the business networking event and raced back to my office. I had to figure out what LinkedIn was, and how I could start connecting with people there. That night, I created a LinkedIn profile. I also began, though I didn't know it then, my digital marketing career.

For the next several weeks, I fully immersed myself into what LinkedIn had to offer. Somewhere during this time, I also joined Twitter and Facebook (figuring, if I was going to invest myself in social media, I might as well go all the way).

I downloaded every eBook, watched every YouTube video, and subscribed to every blog I could find that might help me better understand how to harness digital marketing.

It didn't take very long to see the pattern for success:

In the battle for attention online, the Creators always win.

Sure, there is attention that comes from curating other people's content, and engaging on other people's posts. But the power, influence, and prestige is held by those who put in the work to create educational, entertaining and/or inspirational content.

With this realization came an awful feeling: my last several weeks spent on social media had been a waste of time. I wasn't creating at all, just consuming what others had done.

I had this epiphany sitting at my insurance agency desk on a Friday afternoon. The only logical thing to do was to start a blog and get to work. So I stood up, walked into my boss's office, explained my opinion on creating content, and asked if we could start a blog.

His response was the well-intentioned response lots of bosses give the first time an employee asks to start a blog: "You need to sell more now, not waste time blogging." He wasn't trying to be rude or insensitive. He wanted me to be successful as an insurance salesman. (At the time, none of us realized I was never meant to be an insurance salesman).

However, it was what he said next that changed the course of my life. In an unconsciously visionary moment, my boss followed up with, "But if you want to start a blog in your own name, go right ahead."

And www.RyanHanley.com was born, not as you know it today, but as "The Albany Insurance Professional." At this point I was just a little over a year into my insurance sales career, so by all metrics I still didn't know anything about insurance.

The Albany Insurance Professional blog became a diary of sorts. As I learned a new insurance coverage, I shared my acquired knowledge with the world. One coverage at a time, week after week after week. It became fun to learn about insurance because I got to write about each new coverage I learned on my blog.

Here's the crazy part: *people started to read it*. And not just other insurance professionals, but consumers as well. It took about nine months, but on a random Wednesday in the middle of August, 2010, I received a message through the contact form on my website from a woman looking for homeowners insurance.

She'd been looking for a local insurance provider after a bad experience with one of the big-box direct insurance writers, and she found my blog in a Google search. She'd read a few articles, liked what I had to say, and decided she wanted to buy her homeowners insurance from me.

I was officially a content marketer.

From this point on, I felt like a crack addict for inbound leads. I wanted more and more and more. My every waking thought was about what I could do to set myself apart and attract more leads (In the chapters to come, you will learn all these things, too).

Over the next year, working off my own [social media] platform, I was able to try everything—and I mean *everything*. I didn't have to ask anyone permission to test a new strategy or tactic or platform. Like a teenager who realizes his parents left the liquor cabinet open, I wanted a taste of everything.

Some of it worked and some didn't but, most importantly, the leads kept coming.

Every Monday morning we would have a sales meeting. Part of each meeting was set aside for sharing the highlights of what you had sold the week before, and telling where you got that new piece of business from. With increasing regularity, my report included "The Internet" as the source of my sales.

And, as you would assume, questions started to be asked about how I was able to attract these leads from "The Internet." Thus the inevitable transition began . . .

» From Personal to Corporate Blog

Though I loved creating content for The Albany Insurance Professional blog, there were some barriers keeping me from reaping the full reward the Internet had to offer. The most restricting obstacle focused on the nature of my site itself.

Why was I writing as The Albany Insurance Professional and not my insurance agency? Was I really an insurance agent, or some sort of broker who had to pay an additional fee? Whom did I actually work for? These questions created a disconnect for consumers in the natural process of buying insurance, and it was my belief that disconnect restricted the flow of new leads.

In March of 2011 I convinced ownership that we needed a [company] blog, that we needed to start utilizing social tools, and that WordPress was the solution.

However, after our initial post announcing the switch to a more modern website, we didn't post another blog article for almost eight months, not one. The website just sat there, inactive—mostly due to internal disagreements over how Internet leads would be handled and who would be compensated.

What I didn't realize at the time was that this inaction was setting up the perfect case study in small business Search Engine Optimization (SEO) success. The inaction created a baseline for traffic generation to an inactive website (Visit http://bit.ly/cwbookseo to view charts and more details)

Our inactivity yielded approximately 90 website visits a week. The overwhelming majority of those website visits were to one of two pages: the homepage, or our contact page. Why our homepage or contact page?

Those were the two pages with our address and phone number. The hits were from people that already knew us, and needed either directions or a way to contact us. During this time period, we wrote *zero* new business from the website.

This was not the revenue-generating machine I had envisioned when I updated and relaunched our website. Which is how I learned a valuable lesson (a lesson we'll discuss more later in the book):

Inactivity destroys profitability online.

Picture me banging my head off a wall for eight-plus months. That's what I would do every week when I checked our Google Analytics and stared at a flat, lifeless line.

The website line of death.

» An Adrenaline Shot to the Heart

In December, 2011, fed up with the lack of results, I went back to ownership and pleaded my case to begin blogging on our corporate site. Either they were sick of me putting all online work into my own website or just sick of me bothering them about it. No matter why, they relented, and agreed that it was time to see what I could do.

Remember, our website is dead at this point. We are getting close to zero traffic from consumers who aren't already clients. We need to do something drastic to bring this website back to life.

What does triage look like in terms of digital marketing?

Content. Lots and lots of high quality, useful content.

So I came up with a plan to deliver my adrenaline shot. I would answer 100 Insurance Questions in 100 Days via YouTube video, and embed those videos on our site.

What could turn Google on more than a massive amount of extremely useful and helpful content utilizing their own tool?

As I would find out, nothing.

» The Questions Matter

The secret to getting found Online is creating content that aligns with how consumers actually search.

From my work creating content as The Albany Insurance Professional site, (the old title of RyanHanley.com) I knew that, in order for the "100 Questions Answered in 100 Days" video series to work, I had to be answering questions that insurance consumers actually searched for. So for the entire month of December, 2011, I asked every person I came in contact with—in any capacity—one simple question:

"If you could only have one insurance question answered, what would it be?"

I emailed clients, friends and family. I posted to Facebook, LinkedIn and Twitter. I asked every client that came in the office.

In total I received 147 responses. I pared them down to 100 questions by removing the duplicates and off-the-wall questions, ones that weren't really relevant to what I was trying to do.

I had my list of questions, phrased exactly as insurance consumers asked them.

Collecting the questions and phrasing them exactly as they were asked was one of the most important aspects of this process.

This is because professionals (of every industry) talk about their business in a very specific way, like masters of a craft. As a master of your craft, your brain bypasses things that experience has taught you are unimportant.

But that's exactly why we can't cheat and ask the questions ourselves. As masters-of-craft, we may realize that something is unimportant or unnecessary, but that doesn't mean our potential clients share this wisdom.

When our potential clients need to find a solution to a problem in a certain industry, they are going to search Google *with the understanding they have, using the phrasing they use.* Our (master) phrasing is going to be different from their (consumer) phrasing, and when it comes to capturing leads online, all we should care about is the phrasing consumers type into Google.

So now that I had our 100 questions, phrased in terms used by our clients— *the phrasing they will type into Google*— it was time to get to work.

» The Nuts and Bolts

I know this chapter is my personal story, but let's take a second to explain the nuts and bolts of this process. If you take away any tactic or strategy from this book, repeating some form of my "100 Questions Answered" project is the one to take away.

The trick here is that you don't just answer the questions willy-nilly. You answer each question in 90 seconds or less on video, and you are NOT—I repeat, NOT—going to use any technical industry barf language that your potential customer is not going to understand.

The key to using video is keeping the answer short. This is how you connect and add value, while respecting the viewers' time.

Each question acts as the title of both the video and the blog post on your website. Using 350-500 words packaged around the video, the blog becomes a search-optimized, keyword-rich solution center that provides undeniable value in the form of answered questions.

These videos, collected together over time, become a completely radical new form of FAQ page or Frequently Asked Questions page. This is you, business professional, sitting in front of a camera, delivering knowledge in casual, conversational language, as if sharing a glass of scotch with an old friend.

This is you, business professional, showing that you're a human with a personality, not someone spewing the standard corporate double-speak that most companies hide behind on their website.

The purpose of this "Questions Answered" strategy is to create a very searchable, highly valuable resource in a short period of time. The execution of this plan should take no more than 30 minutes a day. Batch video creation into one day a week. Use your iPhone and a simple lavaliere microphone for better sound.

If you have a Mac computer, iMovie is a great resource for editing, but there are plenty of free and/or inexpensive options for editing video available in the market. At the time of writing this (2014) I recommend Screenflow for Mac and Camtasia for PC.

» The Results

Day number one, January 2nd, 2011:

There was an immediate spike in traffic on The Albany Insurance Professional. This makes sense, because we were sharing the 100 Questions Answered articles throughout social media and email to generate attention. We finally had content for people to view (beyond our address and phone number) and some of clients and friends did.

But it's not the immediate spike in traffic that interests me personally, nor should you, the reader, be impressed. Sharing our first post for the first time on different social platforms brought attention just because people like to see what we're all about. It would be easy for me to say that Google loves the "100 Questions Answered" video series, and then show you results that are tainted by social media activity.

Here's the thing. After the first week, it was obvious our social media connections and email subscribers were getting burnt out. So we stopped promoting every new video.

You would think that would mean significantly less traffic to our site. But something crazy happened (or seemingly crazy at the time) . . .

Our traffic just kept going up.

We were getting an increasing number of views per video, despite not promoting the videos the way as we did at the beginning of the campaign.

I was learning first-hand the power of long-tail keywords (*creating content targeting phrases versus single keyword terms*).

As a quick note, Neil Patel, co-founder of the website analytics tools Crazy Egg and KISSmetrics, recently shared that 91 percent of the over 260,000 visitors he received to his personal website, QuickSprout.com, come by way of long-tail keywords. We're going to dive deeper into long-tail keywords later in the book. For now, make a mental note that optimizing your content with *phrases* (such as "What is New York Short-term Disability Insurance?") instead of *keywords* (like "Disability Insurance") is an extremely powerful way of winning the attention of qualified leads via Google Search.

In the insurance industry, we have some pretty stiff competition for search engine real estate. Names like GEICO, AllState, State Farm and Nationwide spend billions of dollars on advertising. At the time I began the "100 Questions Answered" campaign, our entire web presence (including site design, hosting, graphics and email marketing) cost us less than $1,500 a year. But here's the surprise: because the mega-companies battle so fiercely for keywords, almost none go after any type of long-tail keyword phrases (and this goes for every industry).

This means opportunity is there, for those willing to put in the work.

» Money Talks

So we received an increase in website traffic from the "100 Questions Answered" campaign.

So what? We don't make payroll on our website, right?

You want to know if we made any sales, and you want to know how much.

Fair enough.

The answer is, during the 100 days in which we were publishing new videos, we produced $4,975 in net new business revenue—not total sales— but net revenue to our business directly attributable to the "100 Questions Answered" campaign.

Nice. Still, your mind is most likely NOT blown by that figure. But remember, that's not all the revenue we produced as a business. The "100 Questions Answered" campaign was an activity *in addition* to everything else we'd always done to produce revenue. We *added* $4,975 in revenue that we wouldn't have otherwise realized. In terms of revenue growth, this meant a 9 percent increase in revenue over the 100 days in which we ran the campaign. You'd take 9 percent growth in revenue over the next 100 days, wouldn't you?

Let's break this down a little further.

During the "100 Questions Answered" campaign, I tracked the time I spent creating and publishing each new video and the corresponding blog post. At the end of the 100 days, I was averaging 18 minutes from camera turned on to finished video and published blog post.

That's 18 minutes a day for 100 days and a total of 1,800 minutes of work or 3.75 work days. This means, with less than a week's worth of work, we were able to grow our revenue by 9 percent.

As an hourly rate, we were making $165 an hour. That's significant. Needless to say, from this point on, I was sold on the power of content marketing and what it could do for my business.

→ The Rub

Here's the rub. If you, at any point in reading this book, begin to say to yourself, "This won't work in my industry," or "My boss would never approve something like this," go ahead and slap yourself across the face. It's time to wake up and stop making excuses.

Content marketing works. It doesn't matter who your boss is (we'll address getting buy-in later), what product you're selling, or who you're selling to.

Sure, there are obstacles that are going to delay success in some instances. It took me a year and a half of blogging on my own website (www.ryanhanley.com) before I was allowed to blog on the corporate website.

And so, with my story out of the way, our journey—**your journey**—begins.

What is content marketing?

New to content marketing?

You're reading the right book. I'm a firm believer that, in order to be successful in any endeavor, we must build upon a solid base. In this case, we're answering the very first question marketing managers, sales managers and business owners have when looking to grow their business online:

"What is Content Marketing?"

If you're considering marketing your business or brand online, then you've certainly come across the term "content marketing" before. And it's very possible you've read something about "content marketing" being important to successful online marketing.

Before we start building our content marketing strategy, it's necessary to understand what content marketing actually is.

According to Wikipedia, *"Content marketing is any marketing format that involves the creation and sharing of media and publishing content in order to acquire customers."*

Our definition: Creating and publishing media to acquire customers.

That's a good start.

According to Copyblogger Media, *"Content Marketing means creating and sharing valuable free content to attract and convert prospects into customers, and customers into repeat buyers."*

Our definition: Creating and publishing free media to acquire customers and repeat buyers.

That's better.

According to the Content Marketing Institute, *"Content marketing is a marketing technique of creating and distributing valuable, relevant and consistent content to attract and acquire a clearly defined audience –*

with the objective of driving profitable customer action."

Our definition: Creating, publishing and distributing media content to acquire targeted, profitable customers and repeat buyers.

Now we have it.

What is Content Marketing?
Content marketing is the process of creating, publishing and distributing media content to build an audience of targeted, profitable customers and repeat buyers.

Great.

But what does this definition mean in application?

Educate. Entertain. Inspire.

We create blog posts, videos, podcasts, images and other forms of rich media to educate, entertain and/or inspire our target audience.

When we've created enough value for our audience, with enough regularity to build trust, our brand easily stands out from the competition. The result? Target customers who have convinced themselves our solution is the perfect solution for their problem.

» Does Content Marketing Work?

Now that we have a working definition for content marketing and baseline understanding for its purpose in our digital marketing strategy, the next logical question is, "Does content marketing work?"

Considering that you've spent money on and invested time into reading a book on content marketing, let's assume that you, at a minimum, believe content marketing can work, if you're not already experiencing some level of success.

» The Content Marketing Tipping Point

As new Google algorithm updates constantly change the rules, and social media sites like Facebook force businesses to pay to reach their own customers, it seems that every SEO and social media consultant has now become a "content marketer."

Whether you're the CMO or CEO, a tipping point has been reached, creating pressure to figure out if content marketing will work for your business.

Despite having purchased this book, you may still be on the fence about content marketing. It's not hard to see why. There's so much misinformation online about what content marketing is and how it works.

So the most important question remains: *Does content marketing work?*

The horrible answer? It depends.

Now, after reading this book, "It depends" will be tilted much more in your favor. But that's only if you let go of the "publish and pray" method implemented by far too businesses attempting to DIY content marketing. Not having a content marketing strategy will not grow your business.

This book is going to help you build that strategy. But first, let's talk about why strategy is so important.

» When Content Marketing Works

Content marketing done right works every time.

In a 2014 study done by the Content Marketing Institute, 42 percent of B2B (Business to Business) companies consider their content marketing efforts effective, up from 36 percent the year prior.

Why the increase in content marketing effectiveness?

> » 73 percent responded that their company added a dedicated professional overseeing their content marketing strategy.

> » 44 percent responded that their company created a documented content strategy.

These results are a sign that the marketplace is starting to take content marketing seriously.

Does content marketing work?

Yes.

Content marketing works when you treat the process as a revenue-generating business function and commit the necessary resources for success.

Content marketing is work. There is no easy way to success. However, there is a path to success, a battle plan, if you will. *Content Warfare* is that battle plan.

Those organizations who follow the battle plan outlined in the pages to follow and put in the work, will reap the benefits of growth and market share in years to come. Markets may change. The value from the customer/client relationships you build won't.

The Culture of Belief in Content Marketing

"The cost of being wrong is less than the cost of doing nothing" ~
Seth Godin

Chances are, the toughest barrier you'll encounter on your journey to winning the battle for attention online won't be a barrier in the physical sense at all. The barrier that will shut your efforts down and ensure failure before you ever get started isn't technical expertise, organizational bandwidth or the budget. That barrier is **belief.**

Belief is a tricky topic. As human beings, we enter every situation with a preconceived belief about what something is or how something should be done. This is especially true in business.

The strongest and most wide-spread belief holding organizations back from content marketing success is the idea that the way business has always *been* done is the way it should always *be* done. Content marketing in its digital form is not a native belief for most small businesses, except for those built within the digital world.

The 'status quo' organizations don't believe in the power of content marketing. However, the number of businesses who've taken the plunge into content marketing to grow their business increases every year. According to blogging.org, 35 percent of US businesses were actively blogging in 2012. Today, according to eMarketer, that number is more than 40 percent.

The holdouts use ROI (return on investment) as an excuse for their lack of action.

Return on Investment: *A profitability measure that evaluates the performance of a business by dividing net profit by net worth.*

The ROI argument against content marketing essentially states that content marketing lacks a true and measurable ROI, and is therefore not worth pursuing versus traditional sales tactics. The argument is an empirical crutch, the classic armchair quarterback decision: all opinion, having taken zero risk.

Anyone who has ever tried to convince a nonbeliever that content marketing is important to business knows that the nonbeliever has many excuses to not even start. So the issue becomes: how do we sell content marketing within an organization of nonbelievers?

» Developing a story for content marketing belief

Convincing the stakeholders within your organization that content marketing is vital to the growth and success of the overall marketing strategy can be very difficult. (Seriously, it took me almost two years). But if there is anything that I learned from my own struggle to develop belief in content marketing, it's that building your pitch as *story* will yield much more fruit than a fact sheet.

There's an overwhelming amount of proof available in the form of web traffic and smart technology adoption rates that we could throw at nonbelievers to convince them content marketing works.

Let's run through that statistical evidence:

XLI

Companies who believe in inbound marketing (which encapsulates content marketing, social media marketing, email marketing, etc.) enjoy 54 percent more leads generated by inbound tactics than companies who focus on traditional paid marketing.

According to the Hubspot State of Inbound report, which surveys the inbound marketing industry on a yearly basis, marketers who have prioritized blogging are 13 times more likely to enjoy positive ROI. A piece of this success comes from dedication and consistency: 82 percent of marketers who blogged daily acquired a customer using their blog, as opposed to 57 percent of marketers who blogged monthly.

We've already heard this story in my 100 Questions Answered campaign. But in reality, for every theory that we present as a proponent, there are diametrically opposed theory that can be thrown out by opponents (*most of which will not seem logical or reasonable*). Company stakeholders do not have to give logical or reasonable reasons for their opposition to content marketing (especially when you report *up* to them). Most of the reasons against content marketing are based on emotion and misconceptions.

If you're fighting for content marketing inside your organization, don't let this irrationality frustrate you. Decision makers have the right and prerogative to believe what they will. Instead of trying to beat down irrational arguments from nonbelievers with facts that won't matter to them anyway, try telling a story. Take nonbelievers through the entire content marketing journey, to a future world where content is a crucial part of their business.

As you'll learn with each section of this book, success starts and ends with your story.

» A Tale of Content Marketing

The traditional story structure has three acts. This is also the story template for selling content marketing to those who would block your path.

The First Act

The first act of our content marketing story is the setup. This is where we establish the main characters, their relationships with each other and the project, as well as the role each will play. The setup is the world as we know it today. We paint this picture as close to reality as possible. Don't be tempted to make the current situation seem worse than it really is. The stakeholders who've worked to build the business to where it is today will either **1)** tune you out or **2)** prepare to tear your recommendations apart in an effort to defend their own work.

We're not pitching content marketing as solution at this point, just setting the table for content marketing as a potential option moving forward.

The Second Act

The second act of our story is the confrontation. Now is when we begin to expose areas of our business where there is currently weakness that content marketing could strengthen, on both a short-term and long-term basis. During the confrontation phase, it's vitally important to show each stakeholder how change—the implementation of content marketing—will impact their role inside the organization.

We want to address the potential concerns associated with content marketing head on. Show where content marketing will create more work, where new technology is going to be needed, where new or repositioned staff may be needed. Show the effort and change involved with developing and implementing a content marketing strategy. Be completely transparent. Most of the stakeholders will have gone through organizational change before; to blow past potential challenges would discredit your argument.

It's this confrontation phase where the idea of **implementing a content marketing strategy** becomes real. Use examples from other organizations, even competitors and peer organizations currently using content marketing to grow their business (You can straight steal my 100 Questions Answered campaign; in fact, I'm hoping that you will). Transparency and honesty will go a long way to reduce the barrier that stakeholders present to accepting content marketing as part of their business. Most of the time, reluctance in adopting a content marketing strategy stems from naiveté and misunderstanding.

Lastly, we want to use the second act of this story to describe the potential eventualities of not establishing a content marketing strategy. What will competitors be able to do that your business will not? How does inaction affect brand strategy? What is the impact on acquisition goals (i.e. subscribers, leads, contacts, sales)? We want to show conflict. Act Two is all about comparing implementation cost vs opportunity cost.

The Third Act

The third act of our story is the resolution. We've set the stage, unlocked the doors, and now it's time to walk through. Act Three is where we show stakeholders what happens when content marketing works. Now we pull out projections on growth, subscriber rates, referrals, brand awareness and whatever other metrics electrify the spine of those who would give you the keys to the car. Act Three is our future with content marketing.

The third act must include case studies. Peer organizations who've had success work great; competitor organizations already executing a content marketing strategy (especially competitors in your local market) work even better.

If you can't answer the question, "Who else is doing this?" Don't move into the third act. This question will absolutely be asked, and being prepared with multiple examples will grease a lot of wheels.

In addition to case studies and facts supporting your argument for content marketing, create goals. Depending on how much marketing your organization has done in the past, setting marketing goals for a activity you've never done before may seem arbitrary and, to a certain extent, these goals may indeed *be* arbitrary. However, what presenting goals shows is that you're serious about the work.

Use your knowledge from Acts One and Two—your organization's current state, the implementation costs and opportunity costs of content marketing—as a baseline for setting realistic goals. Then use some intuitive and instinct.

You wouldn't be pushing for content marketing inside your organization if you didn't believe it could help your business grow (at least, I hope you wouldn't). My advice for Year One is to make your goals achievable, but productive and profitable. Once you get a feel for what you're doing, once you've found your audience and understand how to tell your story (this could be three months or three years from now) seek out stretch goals.

» Formatting Your Story

Now that we understand what our content marketing story is going to look like, it's time to talk about what it's going to sound like. When developing any story, it's important to understand where to spend your time to keep the audience's attention (in this case your boss). Act One should be very short; everyone sitting in the room has a good feeling of what the baseline looks like. All we're trying to do in Act One is confirm that everyone's on the same page. No one is going to believe in content marketing based on Act One alone; move on quickly once a consensus of the current state of the business is reached.

Act Two is going to be where we spend the most time developing the foundation of belief in stakeholders. We take as much time as is reasonable to hash out all the misunderstandings, questions, concerns, and issues in the room that prevent moving forward with content marketing. Different stakeholders are going to see things from different angles; everyone is going to be protecting their little piece of the kingdom. Going in with the understanding that this conflict exists will help you focus in on problems and get to Act Three.

Act Three will be just a little longer than Act One, but shorter than Act Two. If you properly set the stage in Act One and address barriers in Act Two, stakeholders should be drooling over the results content marketing can provide by the time you get Act Three. Now all you need to do is set the hook.

» Belief Will Come Slowly

Consider Everett Rogers theory on the *Diffusion of Innovations*. This theory seeks to explain how, why, and at what rate new ideas and technology spread through cultures. Everett Rogers, a professor of rural sociology, XLV popularized the theory in his 1962 book *Diffusion of Innovations*. Visualize your standard bell curve. Starting from the left, the first 2.5 percent representation Innovators, these are the people who not only embrace new ideas but seek them out. The next segment is the Early Adopters, then comes the Early Majority, Later Majority and finally the Laggards.

This is the path of belief your story will travel in its journey to achieve stakeholder buy-in. Some will get it immediately; others will need more time. Mentally prepare yourself for this to happen, and don't let laggards frustrate you and derail your efforts. Not all stakeholders will start their journey to belief in content marketing at the same place.

Even if you spin a tale that George R.R. Martin *(Game of Thrones)* would be proud of, belief in content marketing may come slowly. All that you're looking for in telling this story is for stakeholders to *begin* to believe, and to give you the opportunity to start your work. But don't be surprised by future questioning and second-guessing: it's going to happen. But taking the time to tell your content marketing story ensures that you won't have the plug pulled on your effort at the first sign of trouble.

For most organizations, taking on an initial content marketing strategy is work *in addition* to everything already done within the organization. Embrace the process, don't get frustrated by naysayers, and put in the work. Planting the seeds of content marketing success today will reap huge benefits in the future.

In order to accomplish anything worth accomplishing, there must first be belief.

XLVIII

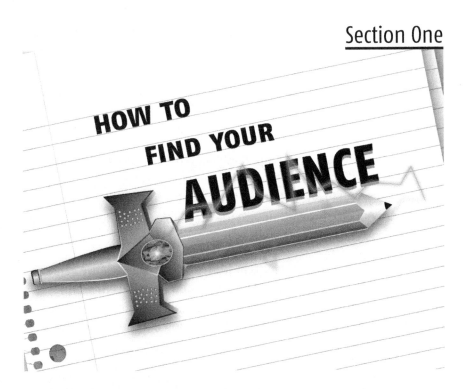

HOW TO FIND YOUR AUDIENCE

"I don't believe in elitism. I don't think the audience is this dumb person lower than me. I am the audience." ~ Quentin Tarantino

In 2008, Kevin Kelly, co-founder of *Wired* Magazine, published a seemingly straight-forward post on his blog titled "1,000 True Fans." In this post, Kelly defines a True Fan as "someone who will purchase anything and everything you produce. They will drive 200 miles to see you sing. They will buy the super-deluxe re-issued hi-res box set of your stuff even though they have the low-res version. They have a Google Alert set for your name. They bookmark the eBay page where your out-of-print editions show up. They come to your openings. They have you sign their copies. They buy the t-shirt, and the mug, and the hat. They can't wait till you issue your next work. They are True Fans."

True Fans serve as the bedrock of our audience. Upon the foundation of these True Fans is our entire empire built. True Fans will serve as your generals in the battle for attention online, because they believe the value is not just in your products or services, but in you the person (or company).

True Fans believe that, in supporting you and your work, they are making an investment in themselves. They believe that their support facilitates the creation of future value you could not possibly create without their support. They're zealots, fanatics, and diehards, and to build an audience that will grow your business, you must build your audience of True Fans first.

This is the mistake so many companies make. They believe in the "Field of Dreams" marketing theory: "*If you build it, they will come.*" Unfortunately, reality doesn't follow theory in this case. Only those who build their audience first will survive the inevitable "Dip" that Seth Godin so famously explained in his book by the same name.

As Kevin Kelly explains, the genius of True Fans is in their relative value. Each True Fan has far more value to the creator than less-connected audience members do. True Fans can provide this value in three ways: **1)** by purchasing more per person; **2)** by spending directly so the creator keeps more per sale; and **3)** by enabling new models of support.

2   Kelly's outline of the benefits of a True Fan are geared towards creators looking to make a living from their art. (The second benefit doesn't have a directly applicable correlation for brands not in the art business). For brands outside the art world looking to grow revenue from the accumulation of True Fans, we must make a few adjustments.

The first benefit, that True Fans are going to spend more per person than audience members less connected to your brand or message, applies directly to growing your business.

We're going to adjust the first benefit slightly to go beyond just purchasing more per sale, to include purchasing more total items you sell. True Fans are more likely to purchase the scope of all products and services you offer. Where a less-connected audience member is only going to buy the single product or service they need, a True Fan wants everything you offer. They don't just buy their favorite movie in the series: they buy the box set, action figures, and tickets to the next convention.

The third benefit, (and final adjustment to Kevin Kelly's original benefits), of True Fans is their willingness to amplify your message through unsolicited sharing within *their* own audiences. Out of the three True Fan benefits, this can ultimately be the most valuable to the growth of your business. True Fans are the catalyst of viral spread.

As Jonah Berger said in his book, *Contagious: Why Things Catch On*, "Virality isn't born; it's made." By no means am I saying the goal of our content should be "Going viral." But by understanding *why* things go viral, we can better position our content to spread among the communities that would potentially buy our products and services.

Berger goes on to outline six primary drivers of viral content:

Social Currency (making people feel that they are cool insiders)

Triggers (everyday reminders of an item or idea)

Emotional Resonance (making people want to share the experience with friends)

Observability (that is, a highly *visible* item will "advertise" itself)

Usefulness (people like to share practical or helpful information); and

Storytelling (embedding a product or an idea within a narrative to enhance its power).

3

In theory, producing content which places all six of these tumblers in line does not seem difficult. However, the practice of this concept is extremely challenging. The trick is to view virality in relative scale to your business need. This is the concept of "relative virality," or, the rapid spread of content *within a niche.*

To be honest, your business does not need one million views of your latest YouTube video in order for that video to create revenue. In truth, ten thousand, one thousand, or even a hundred views may be all you need, depending on the market you serve.

Disseminating your content is where you will need help.

You can create the snowball and give it the initial kick down the mountain. But in order for the snowball to reach self-sustaining momentum, it's going to need help. This where True Fans come in.

Your True Fans are the first to see your new content because they're subscribed to your RSS feed, email list, and/or social media. True Fans, having already bought into your message, don't need to be convinced your content is worth sharing. They've already developed the "Emotional Resonance," as Jonah Berger puts it, to click your social sharing buttons, forward the email, or even create their own content in response to yours.

The more True Fans you develop within your audience, the more initial momentum gets applied to your content. Your True Fans share to their True Fans, who share to their True Fans—and down the line your message spreads.

So the question becomes, "How many True Fans does my business need?"

Kevin Kelly titled his article "1,000 True Fans," but that figure is completely arbitrary. Kelly admits that one thousand is a nice, round, seemingly-achievable number of True Fans, but that it is in no way "the rule." **True Fan accumulation, cultivation and activation is the goal;** hitting an arbitrary number is not.

From my own experience for a local small business, the number of True Fans can be as low as two to three hundred, and still achieve massive success. For a regional or national mid-sized business, or a company selling through the Internet to a wider audience, the number may be three to five thousand True Fans.

For the purposes of winning the battle for attention online, the number should not be the goal. The goal is putting the processes in place to build your audience base of True Fans.

True Fans

We now understand the importance of building a foundation of True Fans. However, before we can begin the discussion of how to attract True Fans, we must first figure out who they are.

Do you know who your True Fans are?

Please don't answer, "People who buy my product," or "People who subscribe to my newsletter," or (heaven forbid) "People who follow me on social media." Wrong, wrong, wrong.

These are audience members, but they are not True Fans. *Not everyone who buys from you is a True Fan.*

Marinate on that thought for a second. In your business-owner, salesperson, marketer mind, it's easy to confuse customers with True Fans. Here's the difference: Customers buy things from you, but True Fans help you grow your business. It's possible for a customer to not be a True Fan, and it's also completely possible for a True Fan to *not* be a customer (though less likely).

Last week, I was flying home from Grand Rapids, Michigan, after speaking to a group of insurance agents. The only coffee place I could find in the airport was Starbucks and, because I'm completely addicted to coffee, I bought a cup, even though I don't particularly care for Starbucks. That's it: that's the end of the story. I bought the coffee, and became a customer of Starbucks. But I'm not a True Fan.

Now if that coffee shop had been a Dunkin Donuts, my coffee purchase would most likely have been followed by an Instagram photo of me in the airport with my Dunkin Donuts coffee, sharing solid, low-budget travel wisdom and the hashtag #runondunkin. Why would I ever do such a thing? What's the point?

I love Dunkin Donuts coffee. I'm a True Fan, and I want my world to know, just like I hashtag my love for the Buffalo Bills #GoBills whenever I get a chance—even if it's not necessarily relevant.

5

Ryan Hanley

Customers buy your product, Subscribers receive your newsletter, and Connections follow you on Google+, Facebook, Twitter or whatever social media platform you've built a presence on.

Sure, you want more customers, subscribers and connections, but you shouldn't build a content strategy around these groups. These groups are just too broad.

To grow your audience, you must serve one person: your True Fan. By doing this, you're able to focus your efforts on developing relationships with people who believe in what you're doing. Everyone else will fit themselves into the appropriate slot or slots (i.e. Customer, Subscriber, Connection).

The work is growing your audience one person at a time.

Don't freak out.

I know the idea of growing your audience one person at a time is contrarian. Ambitious readers may find it downright silly.

But we can't be everything to everyone. Google has killed the generalist, and in terms of searching for solutions online, in many ways the world is better for it.

Google Has Killed the Generalist (and Why We All Need More True Fans)

"Google is looking for the authority," said Brian Clark, founder of the content marketing thought-leadership center, Copyblogger.com, during an interview with Eric Enge, founder of Stone Temple Consulting.

It's incredibly difficult to become an authority on a topic. I've been writing about content marketing and Google Plus for more than three years, and I'm just starting to see some significant traction. That's after 39 months of focused effort.

If, instead of focusing, I had also talked about email marketing, and Facebook and Twitter and other random feelings I had on a given day, I'd be nowhere near building a significant audience on any of these topics.

Google Doesn't Believe in the Generalist.

On Google's 'About' Page, their mission statement reads, "Google's mission is to organize the world's information and make it universally accessible and useful."

Next, we drill down even farther to the Google company philosophy, which Google entitles "Ten Things We Know to Be True." The number two item reads, "It's best to do one thing really, really well."

If Google has gone through the effort of creating a list of ten things they know to be true and placing on that list the statement, "It's best to do one thing really, really well," essentially preaching the gospel of specialization, is there any reason to believe that their search product would in any way appreciate your generalist content?

No.

Google does NOT appreciate the generalist online (with the exception of mega media sites like Huffington Post, which can't really be considered generalists due to the amount of content they create on every topic).

Let's take the quick example of your average independent insurance agency, which writes personal and small-to-mid-sized commercial lines policies, as well as some life insurance and health insurance.

Common practice would be to create pages for each of these products. We're talking fifty different products spanning a hundred different industries.

That average, independent insurance agency—if it puts in the work—may eventually be able to rank high on the search engine for some general insurance-related terms. But here's the dirty little secret most Search Engine Optimization (SEO) and content marketing professionals don't tell their clients:

General search terms yield shit in terms of actual sales.

Great for traffic, terrible for revenue.

Why?

8 General search terms are where people begin their journeys to purchase, not where they finish.

In a 2013 study done by Pardot, a Salesforce.com company, 98 percent of B2B (Business to Business) buyers refine their searches from general to focused throughout the buying process. More than 70 percent of B2B buyers return to search engines 2-3 times before making a buying decision.

Google knows this. The number one item on their "Ten Things We Know to Be True" list: "Focus on the user and all else will follow."

It's great to rank for the generalist terms, as did my former insurance agency, "Albany Auto Insurance." But the money comes from specific, long-tail search terms directed at pages which position your business as a specialist.

To harness the true power of content marketing, we must work to be our customers' *last* search—not their first.

If long-tail keywords produce targeted search traffic, which consistently converts into leads at a higher rate, why isn't every company online focused on long-tail?

The fault is often a reluctance to give up traditional Internet marketing KPI (key performance indicators), such as website traffic (though, sometimes, the problem is simple naiveté). We're going to dive into long-tail keywords in a later chapter. But for now, understand that our goal is not to become the generalist working to attract the most website traffic. Rather, aspire to be the specialist: seek to please one specific person.

We're not Googling for generalists.

The real reason Google has killed the generalist lies in why consumers visit Google Search in the first place.

We don't go to Google unless we have a problem, a question, or a need. *In which of those categories is the Internet generalist the most valuable resource?*

None.

My sister-in-law used to get back pain—often. Anyone who has dealt with consistent, nagging back pain knows what a life-sucking ailment it can be. Fed up with constant, fruitless visits to doctors and chiropractors, my sister-in-law took to Google in search of a solution.

A former Division I athlete, she was looking for a solution that she herself could take part in. Lo and behold, in searching "How to fix your own back," the very first search result yielded FixYourOwnBack.com. (For those keeping score, "How to fix your own back" is a long-tail keyword).

After browsing the site for approximately a half hour, reading the articles, testimonials and course outline, my sister-in-law decided that FixYourOwnBack.com was a solution she was willing to try. She paid to become a member and, after a few short months of following the course work, was experiencing consistent relief.

Her experience highlights an excellent example of the magic that is the Internet, and of Google's power to connect problems with solutions.

FixYourOwnBack.com helps people fix their own backs. Duh. Maybe

I'm overstating the obvious here, but FixYourOwnBack.com is NOT FixYourOwnBackLegsShouldersElbowsEtc. How could someone be a specialist in back pain, leg pain, shoulder pain *and* elbow pain? When wearing our "consumer" hats, we understand this concept completely.

In truth, the folks at FixYourOwnBack.com aren't even marketing themselves to *all* back pain. They drill themselves down to just disc injury, stating: "What members to FixYourOwnBack.com receive is an organized, systematic plan of exercises designed to specifically address disc injury."

I'm positive that there are thousands, if not hundreds of thousands, of websites which contain similar information and recommended activities found by my sister-in-law on FixYourOwnBack.com. But by focusing on *just* back pain and, even deeper, on *one specific form* of back pain, FixYourOwnBack.com is able to attract targeted traffic, with a specific problem, at the end of the online search process. Active buyers.

Yet, going back to our independent insurance agent example, the vast majority of agents will list thirty different types of businesses that they write insurance for.

10

Just because you *can* sell many things doesn't mean you *should* market all those things online (at least, not at first).

When consumers go to Google with a problem, question, or need, they want *the best* solution, and they are pissed when a search result doesn't provide the best solution.

So Google doesn't show anything other than what it believes to be the best solution.

Over and over throughout this book, I'm going to bang away at this point: **We market our best solutions online first.** Everything else, we leave to cross-selling and up-selling.

Pick your highest margin product, or the product you most want to sell that you also consider yourself a specialist in. The consumers who need That Thing want to work with The Specialist in That Thing.

No one cares (or believes) that you can do everything. The reason they went to Google in the first place was to find who does The Thing they need, the best. If you're that person or business, then that's all you should write about.

» Self Expression

We've really upheld the idea that True Fans want to like, trust and believe in your business, and that positioning yourself as the specialist in a topic helps attract potential new True Fans in your area of expertise. But there is one more piece to the True Fan puzzle we need to dissect before moving on.

True Fans use your business, your brand and your products as a form of **self-expression.** In a study published by Procedia Social and Behavioral Sciences titled "Brands as a mean of consumer self-expression and desired personal lifestyle," author Pagalea Andreea writes:

"In ancient society, each person had a well-established 'place' in the social hierarchy. This 'place' was attained through birth or by wealth. Nowadays, we can speak about a symbolic role of possessions in consumers' lives. People tend to make inferences about others based on their possessions and behavior. In these circumstances, brands have become instruments of status-signaling that satisfy consumer prevalence of a need for status."

It's natural to market our brand on the merits of its differentiation from the competition's. There are three stages of competency with which marketers do this:

The first is differentiation via *features.* If you were an Internet hosting provider, you might include marketing terminology such as, "Fast, secure connection and guaranteed uptime." Companies who market around features believe potential customers are able to make the leap from features their company provides to the benefits a customer will experience.

The second stage of marketing differentiation focuses on *benefits.* Our Internet hosting company example might now read, "Your website visitors will never hit the back button because your site is loading too slow. Our

11

secure connection increases customer confidence, leading to more sales." This is a much more sophisticated method of marketing differentiation, and removes the need for potential customers to figure out how certain features will benefit them. Additionally, marketing in terms of benefits offered forces a company to think less about itself and more about the customers being served.

The third stage of marketing differentiation is when focus moves beyond features and benefits to *what the brand says* about the people and companies that use it. This type of marketing cannot, does not happen in a short period of time. It's taken companies such as Nike and Apple decades to create brands that don't need to sell features or benefits. These companies can now focus solely on what it *means* to wear Nike shoes, or to create on an Apple computer.

A case study done by Hootsuite, a social media management tool, highlights the success of Tourism Jasper. Tourism Jasper is a marketing organization tasked with promoting tourism to Jasper, Alberta, Canada. The tactical crux of what Tourism Jasper did was to create a campaign, #myjasper, which they promoted through all their digital properties (i.e. blog, social media, email list).

The purpose of the campaign was to provide visitors to Jasper and the Jasper National Park with a means to record and share the dynamic experiences they had there. In the first year of the campaign, the #myjasper went from zero to 10,000 images shared, on platforms such as Instagram, Twitter and Facebook.

What Tourism Jasper did was give evangelists an outlet to use their love for Jasper as a piece of self-expression. We humans have a deep desire to express who we are. Sharing a picture of your experience in Jasper using the #myjasper hashtag said something about you: you're an adventurous nature lover.

The hashtag didn't make Jasper cool (it was cool before the hashtag), just like a hashtag or other medium of self-expression won't make our product or service cool. What the Tourism Jasper case study shows us is that by differentiating our business, brand or product by promoting its use as a form of self-expression, we begin to accumulate—not just awareness or new customers—but True Fans.

By giving visitors to Jasper an outlet, Tourism Jasper didn't have to sell new potential visitors on the features or benefits of Jasper. Their True Fans were acting as a sales force by expressing exactly what visiting Jasper says about you as a person when you visit.

The Connected Generation

At many of the presentations I've given on content marketing over the last few years, an audience member has raised his or her hand and asked the exact same question:

"How do we market to Generation Y?"

This question is always prefaced by some stat or idea about Gen Y's disinterest in building relationships or personal connections with the people and brands they do business with. I've found this to be a very common perception about the habits of the Generation Y consumer with mid-sized and small business owners.

If we believed that Generation Y was truly not interested in building relationships, or found no value in personal connections with the brands they do business with, we would have a huge problem.

Fortunately, I think the idea that Generation Y isn't interested in building relationships with the brands they do business with is complete crap.

What these questioning audience members were really expressing is:
"I have no idea how to harness content marketing or social media, and the idea that an entire generation of consumers are using these tools scares the shit out of me . . . What am I supposed to do?"

This is a question we can work with. This version is honest, and represents a solvable problem. Here's the solution:

Why Generation Y doesn't exist

I'm a member of Generation Y, and most of my friends are members of Generation Y. I can tell you, with conviction, that the consumers of Generation Y are starving for deep relationships and personal connections with the brands they do business with.

But, in order to believe that, you would also have to believe that Generation Y exists.

I do not.

At least, not when I wear the marketer's hat.

For a marketer, there are no such groupings of people as Generation Y or Millennials or Generation X, or even the Baby Boomers.

For marketers, especially marketers specializing in content marketing, these generational groupings have no bearing on how we position our value message.

There are only two generations that matter to us:

The Connected Generation consists of individuals willing and open to communications and building relationships, who ultimately make buying decisions based on digital content and interactions.

The Unconnected Generation is everyone else. Unconnected Generation consumers often require in-person transactions, exhibiting an unwillingness to communicate via email or other digital tools, and general skepticism about the Internet.

Nowhere in these two generations are there any defining characteristics based on the year a person was born.   15

According to the website Socialnomics, the fastest growing population on Facebook is 45-55 year olds; the site further claims that almost 55 percent of this population are now active users on Facebook. That's elder Generation X and younger Baby Boomers . . . on Facebook? Shouldn't they be reading the newspaper, listening to the radio and waiting for the postman to drop off the day's mail?

Isn't that the characterization we lay upon this population?

Explaining why this consumer group is growing on Facebook faster than any other requires accepting the thought that age doesn't matter when it comes to digital adoption.

You either communicate, build relationships, and make buying decisions online and thus become part of the Connected Generation, or you do not . . . whether you're 17, 37 or 67 makes no difference.

» 5 Content Marketing Tactics the Connected Generation Can't Resist

1. Intimacy

The Connected Generation wants to know that there is a human being behind our brand. Building intimacy into our content marketing strategy is actually very easy: Just interject a bit of your personal life. *You have kids?* Mention them. *You like the Buffalo Bills?* Describe your sorrow. *You do homemade taxidermy?* Weird, but I'm sure there are some interesting stories.

The point is that a little bit of personality, a little bit of 'behind the scenes', a little bit of who you are as a person builds intimacy with readers, deepening the relationship the Connected Generation is looking for.

2. Vulnerability / Humility

16   Failure can often be our most powerful content marketing tool. The ability to admit the mistakes we make and help others learn from those experiences shows vulnerability and humility. The authority we're trying to convey through content marketing loses value if we can't admit and be honest about failure. No one believes we are perfect and, by showing vulnerability and humility, we disarm our audience.

When we step off our soapboxes and discuss the years of struggling and learning it took to achieve our expertise, success becomes more attainable to our audience—and we've positioned ourselves as a resource.

3. Rich Media

The Connected Generation wants to build deeper connections with the brands they follow and do business with online, and they understand the medium: a stock photo from Google Images and 450 words of text can only do so much to build relationships. To take relationships deeper, our content needs to move past text to audio, video and slideshows.

Consider adding YouTube videos, a podcast, and/or Slideshare presentations. You can even throw quality ebooks into the mix. These types of larger works show dedication and commitment to your work, a trait the Connected Generation is looking for.

4. Social Proof

Not every piece of content with value to your business will be created by you.

Testimonials, recommendations, and reviews are the Connected Generation's referrals. The testimonials, recommendations and reviews you collect on your own website, as well as on review sites such as Google Local and Yelp, are vital to convincing the Connected Generation that your business is legitimate and trustworthy.

This is called social proof, and it's a must-have component in marketing to the Connected Generation.

5. Feedback

Comments and customer feedback are vital content marketing tools, as they provide a completely different yet equally powerful form of social proof. Comments happen on your blog, on social media outposts like Facebook, Twitter, LinkedIn and Google+, and through email marketing.

17

Comments are truly where the magic happens in content marketing.

Comments are the conversation that used to happen solely across a desk. When the Connected Generation is willing to comment and have conversations with brands, it shows engagement *and* shines a spotlight on the brands being engaged with.

The Connected Generation needs a completely different form of content marketing than we're used to as marketers. The Connected Generation is searching to build relationships through the content they consume.

By transforming our content marketing tactics, we can develop a strategy that Connected Generation consumers cannot resist. And ultimately, these Connected Generation consumers can become the True Fans that will grow your business.

Digitizing the Soul of Your Business

"Your income is directly related to our philosophy, NOT the economy."
—Jim Rohn

As the web evolves, it's only natural for web use to become less mechanical. Marketing tactics such as search engine optimization, social media distribution, email capture and sales funnels will lose their current glamour and take their places alongside all the other marketer's tools.

In many ways, this has already begun. We've moved away from the long, adjective-laden, yellow-highlighter-riddled sales pages that once passed as "online business." Such digital used-car salesman tactics have been replaced with personalized messaging, engagement marketing, and storytelling.

Winning brands are focused on starting conversations with their audiences, rejecting the traditional method of buying audience attention.

Winning brands value customer experience over a slick sales funnel, and the cadence of an authentic human voice over legally-approved corporate jargon.

Our goal today is connection.

Consumers embrace the occasional miscue, and celebrate the raw nature of personalities such as Gary Vaynerchuk, (author of *Crush It* and *Jab, Jab, Jab, Right Hook*). In his own words, Gary explains, "I attract a crowd, not because I'm an extrovert or I'm over the top or I'm oozing with charisma. It's because I care."

I would take Gary Vaynerchuk's example even further. He attracts a crowd because he's built a brand with a soul.

Gary has digitized the soul of his business, and that soul flows through every piece of content he creates. In every YouTube video, podcast interview and live presentation, Gary drips a little more of himself onto the audience's plate, and they eat it up. He's a real person with real passions, desires, and goals for his business (like owning the Jets), and he shares those dreams alongside tales of his personal struggles as a workaholic.

Gary shares authentic, transparent, honest guidance as often as he possibly can. His raw style provides the audience (potential clients/customers) with an open window to the beliefs, culture and style that act as the foundation for his VaynerMedia and Gary Vaynerchuk brands.

During Vaynerchuk's live presentations, such as his famous "Inc. 500" speech, listeners assume Gary Vaynerchuk will drop the "F-bomb" frequently. Most presenters couldn't pull off such language. But Gary incorporates profanity with panache. His stream of obscenities serves a purpose. Gary's provocative language acts as a filter for potential clients and customers who wouldn't be good fits for his business.

In addition to acting as a filter, Gary's in-your-face language and raw guidance have built an almost cult-like following. Believers in Gary Vaynerchuk's style and message wear their support like a badge of honor, similar to the way die-hard sports fans rock their favorite player's jersey to a dinner party.

19

This is the relationship Connected Generation consumers want to experience with the brands they do business with. By digitizing the soul of his business and sharing his raw message through digital and social media, Gary is at once filtering out "Bad Fit" clients and endearing himself to true believers.

Person by person, one at a time, we build our audience of true believers. Here's the catch: we must do this with complete disregard for immediate results. I'm not saying results cannot or should not happen quickly. But the concept of digitizing the soul of your business is a long-game play. If this were the NFL, we'd be establishing the run. If this were a Malcolm Gladwell book, we'd be talking about the first 10,000 hours.

Sure, there are ways to expedite this process. I'm a particularly big fan of the concept known as "Growth Hacking" (we talk in more detail about Growth Hacking in Section III). Though there are specific tactics associated with Growth Hacking, in its purest form Growth Hacking is more a mindset than a tactic. Most relevant to our discussion in this book is the concept of getting ideas in front of your **Product Market Fit (PMF),** the group of people who relate completely to the product offered.

PMF is a simple and sound concept that, at face value, almost sounds easy. But how do you know who your Product Market Fit is, what they look like and what they want, if you don't first understand the soul of your own business? I'm talking about the Simon Sinek "Why" of what you're doing. The Product Market Fit isn't going to be sold on the functionality of your product or service alone. Above all else, your Product Market Fit wants to believe in you and your business.

On the Rogers Innovation Curve, we're talking about the first 2.5 percent of people who will ultimately buy from you. Known as the "Innovators," these are the people who are so in tune with what you're doing they simply do not have any other choice than to buy. You, your business, and your product provide an outlet for their self-expression.

The emotional connection produced by the Product Market Fit can't be captured in features or characteristics. The natural desire your PMF audience feels for your product comes from someplace deeper. They feel it in their guts. That feeling drives both their commitment to your business and their willingness to share their experience.

Doesn't a discount make consumers want to share their experience? Shouldn't amazing features make consumers want to share their experience? Couldn't fantastic customer service make consumers want to share their experience?

Maybe. But deep down, the decision to buy is emotion-driven. In his book *Descartes' Error,* Antonio Damasio, professor of neuroscience at the University of Southern California, argues that emotion is a necessary ingredient to almost all decisions. MRI neuro-imagery shows that, when evaluating brands, consumers primarily use the portions of their brains responsible for emotion versus the portions controlling logic-based thought. Furthermore, according to a study done by Advertising Research Foundation, the emotions determining "Likeability" were the most predictive as to whether or not a brand's advertising campaign would be successful.

Why else would the PMF person stand in line outside the Apple store for days, just to purchase the next generation iPhone? The features aren't so much better than what was previously available. In many ways, the Samsung Galaxy S4 and Android Nexus 5 have more appealing features. There certainly isn't any discount in price. Consumers who wait in those lines pay the highest price the new iPhone will ever cost. Not to mention that the purchasing experience of standing in the weather surrounded by strangers is NOT pleasant, to say the least.

But they do it.

They do it again and again and again, for each new version of Apple's iPhone. These people connect with the soul of Apple, just like every PMF consumer does with the product or service they MUST have. The product matches their desires, their core beliefs. It shows the world who they want to be and how they want to be seen.

For more than a decade, Apple has continued to attract a huge Product Market Fit consumer audience. Could it be that they are so dialed into the soul of their business that it's impossible to confuse what it means to be an iPhone user versus an Android? Yes. Everything Apple does is born out of the soul of their business. Despite Apple's almost indistinguishable user interface from Android, I love my iPhone, and hate the Android phone I owned before it. 21

How could that be? Where does the bias come from? I would argue it's from Apple's ability to digitize the soul of their business into everything they do. It's so clear what Apple represents and who they are: simplicity, efficiency, creativity. Its illogical, but I feel more creative working in front of my Apple MacBook computer than I ever did with a PC. We associate the same values with the consumers who use their products.

This is why you spend the time, resources and energy to digitize the soul of your business. Winning the battle for attention online is about accumulating true believers. Whether you're a business of five, five thousand or five hundred thousand, the more true believers you accumulate, the faster your message will spread.

Digitizing the soul of your business is not easy. If you were looking for easy, then you've purchased the wrong book. This chapter is located near the beginning of this book because the following two concepts are so extremely importance.

» First:

You must provide a deep, soul-filled message your audience can connect with. This is vital to winning the battle for attention online. No one wins attention with tactics alone. The audience must feel something deeper if they're going to stick around.

» Second:

You and the other decision-makers/influencers in your organization must be willing to take initiative to share the soul of your business in your content marketing efforts. If this initiative is missing, the rest of the tactics contained in the forthcoming pages will not work. Then, you'll be pissed at me because you bought a book that couldn't help your business.

22 I've made the case for the concept of digitizing the soul of your business as the path to winning the battle for attention online and long-term growth. Now, let's discuss the mechanics of how we actually do it. These five steps are important exercises, because they will set the tone for the content creation and distribution decisions you'll be asked to make later in the book.

Step One

> *"And the day came when the risk to remain tight in a bud was more painful than the risk it took to blossom." ~ Anaïs Nin*

The first step is to let go of any fear of failure, or anxiety you may have attached to sharing the soul of your business with the world. Creating content which evokes an emotional response from consumers can be uncomfortable. This can be especially true for businesses used to producing content thoroughly whitewashed by classic corporate jargon and legal disclaimers.

There are more than a few reasons why you may feel this fear or anxiety. The key factor I discover over and over again in my consulting work and when speaking to audiences across the country: most organizations have no clue what the soul of their business actually looks like.

The soul of your business is not what you do or what you sell. Nor is it *how* you do what you do, or the people you sell it to. Start by thinking back to your Mission Statement on Day One. Digitizing the soul of your business is the articulation of your core motivation for turning the lights on every day.

On Day One, you believed. You believed in your "Why," and the people who were willing to do business with you on Day One believed as well.

Think back to our discussion on the Connected Generation consumer. These consumers have more options than they could ever need in choosing a vendor for every single product and service they require. Every vendor offers the same relative features and benefits.

The Connected Generation consumer wants to believe in who they do business with. According to a 2013 Brand Engagement Survey done by Gensler, 87 percent of consumers choose brands that match their values, and 71 percent of consumers will not buy from brands whose values go against their own.

23

A skeptic might conclude that these findings present a "Damned if you do, damned if you don't" scenario. It's true. Digitizing the soul of your business will turn off consumers whose values do not match your own. But a more accurate and practical conclusion would be that Connected Generation consumers are sorting themselves into lines of qualified leads, based on values your business is perceived to have.

The soul of your business is not what you believe it to be, but what your customer perceives it to be.

» EXERCISE:

In one sentence, write down why you turned the lights on at your business on Day One. What problem were you trying to solve? Though it would be easy and (quite likely) at least partly true to just write "Money" or "Fame," try to think deeper. For most organizations, products and services may change, revenue streams may change, even ownership structure may change, but the reason they went into business on Day One is the same core reason they remain in business today.

Next, survey your current audience as to what they believe is the core motivation or soul of your business. You can hire a company to do this for you, use DIY tools such as Survey Monkey or just send out an email and ask for responses.

Once you've received a strong enough sample of responses from your audience, compare those answers to what you wrote down. Does your current audience perceive your soul to be what you believe it is?

Digitizing the soul of your business starts with narrowing the gaps between where your belief and your audience's perception currently lie.

Step Two

24

"Your stuff starts out being just for you . . . but then it goes out. Once you know what the story is and get it right—as right as you can, anyway—it belongs to anyone who wants to read it. Or criticize it." ~ Stephen King

It doesn't matter if your business is mobile apps or appetizers, you must find what growth hackers call **Product Market Fit.** According to Ryan Holiday, author of *Growth Hacker Marketing,* "The best marketing decision you can make is to have a product or business that fulfills a real and compelling need for a real and defined group of people—no matter how much tweaking or refining this takes."

Classic interruption-based marketing is predicated on convincing consumers, through gimmicks, pricing schemes and relentless advertising, that they need a product or service. Growth hackers find the Product Market Fit by matching product with audience and repeating the process until the product and its message fit a core audience perfectly. Unfortunately, if you haven't previously shared the values upon which your business is built, your current audience may not be the Product

Market Fit.

» Here's a classic example of this: Instagram didn't start out as Instagram. The founders of Instagram actually began with a mobile check-in app called Burbn. Built on the latest HTML5 code and backed by $500,000 in venture capital from Baseline Ventures, Burbn had all the makings of a would-be winning mobile application. Then co-founders Kevin Systrom and Mike Krieger saw a potentially disturbing trend in the way people were using Burbn: quick social photo-sharing.

So they realigned their business, and Instagram was born. Now, I'm not telling you to realign your business. However, what we learn from Instagram is that your first, or current, audience may understand your potential more than you do. **Listening is crucial.**

This is the moment when the nightmare comes true. People are going to leave. When your message is authentic (not contrived to fit some model you *think* your audience wants), it makes sense that some people will leave.

25

The consumers who leave at this stage have been wasting your time. They don't believe in your business. They're buying on price, features or proximity, and are more than willing to use the vendor next door the moment the price dips a penny below your own.

The realignment of your audience is healthy and natural. Below is an exercise to help you track the realignment of your audience

» EXERCISE:

Have listening processes in place to capture feedback, both from current audience members possibly disgruntled by new messaging, and new audience members enamored by it. Without proper listening mechanisms in place, you won't be able to make the ongoing adjustments necessary to maintain momentum.

At the most basic level, use Google Analytics (and any additional traffic-tracking applications set up on your website). Web traffic is one indicator of who is connecting with which content on your website.

Use brand mention tools, such as Mention.com and Google Alerts, to track who is saying what about your brand.

Create a spreadsheet to track social media shares. Categorize the posts by type of messaging. Capture engagement and feedback on these posts (such as Likes, shares, comments, etc.). There are basic and advanced tools which can help with this as well (such as Buffer App and Sprout Social).

Step Three

"Do what you do best, and link to the rest."—Jeff Jarvis

The transition from traditional interruption advertising to marketing with a deeper message isn't always easy. According to the Content Marketing Institute's 2014 Annual Report, only 44 percent of B2B (Business to Business) content marketers have a documented strategy for content creation and distribution. But whether you're part of this orderly group, or just rely on a series of habits you've developed over time, your processes and priorities are going to change.

The goal in digitizing the soul of your business is deeper: creating more loyal, one-on-one relationships. This means that metrics such as frequency of posting, total web traffic and social media network connection count can lose much of their significance. These metrics are replaced with Outbound Brand Engagement (discussed in the Metrics That Matter chapter), conversion rate and brand mentions, to name a few.

According to the above-mentioned report from the Content Marketing Institute, 73 percent of B2B content marketers are producing more content than they did one year ago. In order to stand out, brands must focus their attention on the media types (text, video, audio, etc.) and distribution platforms (email marketing, social media, etc.) in which they do their best work. The one caveat to this are mega-brands (say the Fortune 1000 members), which have the resources and budget to be everywhere they want.

The rest of us have limited budgets and a finite amount of time to share our message. Even mid-market companies with marketing departments will struggle to connect on every social platform. So don't try (at least, not at first).

As more and more brands begin creating digital content, the spaces where that content is shared (i.e. Facebook, Twitter, your inbox, Google Search) are becoming more cluttered. **The only way to stand out is to create and distribute remarkable, memorable, valuable, useful content for a specific target audience.** This becomes very tough if you're working inside ecosystems where your skills, message and/or product don't fit. True connection with your audience is almost impossible.

In an interview on *Chase Jarvis Live*, Gary Vaynerchuk explained his belief on choosing where to spend your social media efforts. He said: "Audiences scale on every platform. Choose the platform where you do your best work."

By "audiences scale," Gary is saying that any social network has enough potential customers to be potentially worth our time. If you're funny, hang out on Twitter. If you're more cerebral, then Google+ is an option. Awesome at cat gifs? Tumblr and Facebook are the places to be.

27

Social media, in its most general sense, has existed for over two decades. The social media ecosystem is maturing. There aren't as many early adopter opportunities to gain quick momentum on a mass scale, like there were with the launches of Twitter, YouTube, Facebook, etc. Gimmicky tactics and strategies that once amassed enormous social media followings now yield significantly diminished results.

Add in social network throttling of post visibility, such as Facebook has done with their news feed algorithm. (As of the writing of this book, brand-page Facebook posts reached only two to sixteen percent of fans). Even those companies that were able to amass large social media followings struggled to build real connections.

Even if large social media follower counts are an internal metric of success, our success as marketers will not come from these, but rather from our ability to *activate* our audience.

How do we activate an audience? Through focused, one-to-one

relationship-building on a limited number of platforms and media. Your goal is not followers. You need connections, relationships, believers— people who see themselves in the soul of your business.

We don't build these kinds of relationships by blasting our message throughout social media, in emails or YouTube pre-roll advertisements. No, these relationships are built more subtly.

» A great example of this is Hubspot's Email Unsubscribe Video. When you unsubscribe from Hubspot's email newsletter, you're taken to a page with a video. In that video, Dan Sally, an inbound marketing specialist for Hubspot, looks straight into the camera and gives a seemingly-authentic last-ditch plea for the email subscriber to reconsider and stay on the list. That's human. That's real.

That's marketing!

Unlike every other experience someone has unsubscribing from an email list, what this video does is create a human relationship. You're not just unsubscribing from Hubspot, you're unsubscribing from Dan Sally. Hubspot could send people who hit the unsubscribe button a "Sorry to see you go" email or landing page like every other company. No one would ever question them for such a conventional move.

But that's not the soul of Hubspot's business. Their willingness to create a piece of content outside of traditional best practices, content designed solely to build a deeper relationship with their consumers (even those ready to leave), is what activates their audience to stay. Does everyone stay? No. But more stay than stay with Hubspot's competition—those who settle for a generic "Sorry to see you go" message.

» EXERCISE:

Where, in your marketing process, have you built opportunities to build one-to-one relationships? You might be responding to every tweet or comment. You may be adding personalization to emails. You may more robustly use uncut/lightly edited first-person video footage. You may highlight specific audience members in your marketing content.

Make a list of these opportunities, and begin creating content that

28

embodies the soul of your business, personally and directly. The truth is that no single activity is likely to bring overnight success. Your best bet is a mixture of relationship-building tactics.

Step Four

"*Telling purposeful stories is interactive. It's not a monolog. Ultimately, purposeful tellers must surrender control of their stories, creating a gap for the listener(s) to willingly cross in order to take ownership. Only when the listeners own the teller's story and make it theirs, will they virally market it.*" ~ Peter Guber

Nothing happens if your audience is not active and engaged. The audience eager to receive your next message grows your bottom line. So, how do we activate your audience to help digitize the soul of your business?

Let your audience play a role in determining what the soul of your business is, and how you deliver your message. This is one part of Austin Kleon's philosophy to "Show Your Work."

29

In his book, *Show Your Work*, Austin Kleon makes the case for letting your audience behind the curtain of creation. Kleon writes, "Words matter. Artists love to trot out the tired line, 'My work speaks for itself,' but the truth is, our work doesn't speak for itself. Human beings want to know where things came from, how they were made, and who made them. The stories you tell about the work you do have a huge effect on how people feel and what they understand about your work, and how people feel and what they understand about your work affects how they value it."

This is how you activate an audience. **You make them a part of your business by letting them into your world.** This will be different for every business. Kleon is specifically talking to artists in his book, but the advice applies to the business world as well.

This doesn't mean sharing your proprietary, trademarked process for creating whatever widgets you sell. Showing your audience behind the curtain could be as simple as explaining the origin of your company's name, like Wistia (a video hosting company).

The name Wistia is different and unique, and Wistia comes right out and shares that their name is completely made up. They chose the name because it sounded cool, and the domain name was available! This short, seemingly innocuous tale of choosing their name lets customers and fans of Wistia deeper into the company. You can picture the discussion between co-founders Chris Savage and Brendan Schwartz as they rattle off fun-sounding words before landing on Wistia.

Sharing is a small but powerful thing. Cleverly-shot marketing videos show the inner workings of Wistia's office space, making customers feel as if they know the humans behind the software. I know, because I am a customer. Even with no endorsement deal to motivate me, I recommend Wistia as often as I can. There are many video hosting providers, yet there is only one (besides YouTube) that I recommend.

And it isn't just sharing your own work that helps consumers attach themselves to your brand. "Your influences are all worth sharing because they clue people in to who you are and what you do—sometimes even more than your own work," writes Kleon.

The goal in showing your work is to provide consumers with a tangible representation of what your brand (personal and/or corporate) stands for. This way, when you finally ask potential customers to subscribe to your email list, buy your product or refer a friend, consumers feel like they're supporting an organization they belong to, not just some corporation looking for more profit.

Done right, your audience won't feel like they're buying a product. They'll feel like they're supporting a cause.

And that's when the magic happens.

» EXERCISE:

How can you let your audience behind the curtain of your business? What aspects of your business can you share on a regular basis that would allow consumers to feel a deeper connection to what you do?

This is your opportunity to not just tell your audience about the soul of your business, but actually show them. Find activities, moments, even personalities around the office that give your audience a raw feel for how your product is made.

Step Five

"Failure isn't fatal, but failure to change might be" – John Wooden

Digitizing the soul of your business is an abstract concept. I'm asking you to make the intangible tangible, through content you share into a computer or handheld device. It's an uncomfortable concept, because sharing something so intimate elicits judgment and criticism.

When we step outside our comfort circle (that little circle our business operates in every day that is safe and secure, boring and dispassionate), real relationships are made. When we position our business to create emotional connections with consumers, the possibilities are vast and endless. We begin to experience the freight train–like momentum of brand loyalty.

31

We're no longer attracting consumers. We're building an audience.

But I must caution: as success is possible, so is failure. By the sheer nature of "endless possibilities," one of those possibilities must be failure. Prepare for these failures, for as former U.S. Senator and Hall of Fame basketball player Bill Bradley wrote, "Ambition is the path to success. Persistence is the vehicle you arrive in."

Let's look at this from a different angle. I was a football player in high school. I loved it. Pure, raw, uninhibited emotional energy expended at its maximum with no regard for personal safety. You were celebrated for letting go of what a normal societal engagement would consider civilized, by delivering impact with every ounce of force in your being. There are few legal things in life (except perhaps extreme sports and actual war) which can release a euphoric cocktail of dopamine and adrenaline equal to leveling your opponent on the football field.

I was a linebacker (which means my job was to hit people) and I was good (by Upstate New York high school football standards). I could set aside the moral human and let the animal out as easily as turning on the lights. I loved it.

In a game where your job is to deliver impact, your opponent's job is the same. As strange as it might sound, to be successful at football while remaining injury-free, you need accept the fact that you're going to get hit. When you get hit, it's going to hurt, and it's going to happen again.

The worst part? No one cares that it hurts. They consider it part of the job. The inability to take a hit is the barrier to entry. It's a relatively high barrier, which explains why most people don't play football.

At Columbia High School in East Greenbush, New York, despite being a Class AA school, we never had enough players to fill out a roster. Therefore, anyone who could hack it got a spot. All you had to do was survive. All you had to do was understand that you were going to fail, and the only expectation anyone really had was that you would get back up and do it again on the next play.

32

Every year kids would try out because they thought it would be cool to be under the "Friday Night Lights," wearing the gear while a grandstand full of people cheered. Every year these new kids made the same mistake: they became wide receivers or defensive backs (positions with traditionally less contact), and thought they could avoid the impact.

Their mistake was not in strategy, but in conceptual understanding of the game. *Everyone* gets hit. *Everyone* fails. These individuals were so worried about getting lit up by an opponent, they never actually engaged in the game.

The sideline is safe. The sideline is your comfort circle. You will not fail on the sideline. You can stand there, look good, be part of the team, and feel safe. You can look out onto the field and dream of what you "could" do if ever given the opportunity. You can make excuses for why you're not in the game, all the while knowing deep inside that the reason you're not the field is simple: fear.

You're afraid of getting hit. You're afraid of being humiliated. You're afraid of failure.

So, stay on the sideline where it is safe. You won't be hit or humiliated or fail. You won't be criticized for your play; no one will judge your decisions; no one will question you, because they won't even know you're there.

I'm going to assume, because you're reading this book, that you want to be on the field. Maybe you feel like you're currently on the sideline. Maybe you feel like you're on the field, but failing too often. If either of these scenarios are the case, it's most likely because you're playing the content marketing game too safe.

When you play it safe, no one cares what you're up to. No one wants to know what you're doing or what you have to say. Your comfort circle is safe and that's great, but no one is going to be inspired by your safe content. Your safe content is making you a commodity.

» Let's look at this from inside an industry I'm very familiar with: the insurance industry. Specifically, let's look at the insurance industry's second largest writer of auto insurance, GEICO. According to a report published by Nomura Equity Research, in 2012 GEICO spent over $1.1 billion dollars on advertising, the highest among every insurance carrier in America. The report goes on to say, "For a commoditized product, low cost and effective marketing are keys to share gain."

33

GEICO's 2012 results would bear out the truth in this statement. In 2012, GEICO grew in all 50 states, including a 12.6 percent median growth rate in their top 10 states, compared to the 4.1 percent of direct-writing competitor Progressive Insurance, who spent only $526 million on advertising during the same period.

It would seem, based on these statistics, that GEICO's epic ad spending and creative commercials with lizards and cavemen and frogs is a strategy for success. However, in a study done by The Hanover Insurance Group, nearly 60 percent of consumers who had purchased insurance through a direct channel 10 or more years ago reported switching back to an independent insurance agent because they wanted more value.

Commenting on the study, Mark R. Desrochers, president of personal lines insurance at The Hanover Insurance Group, stated, "This research demonstrates that consumers really value the advice provided by independent agents and the personal relationships they build with their customers. The majority of respondents said their number one reason for switching from a direct insurance provider was to have someone to guide them through their insurance buying decisions. Clearly trust and expertise are important to consumers."

I take these two data points—GEICO's ability to grow based on price-driven advertising, versus 60 percent of direct insurance consumers returning to independent insurance agents inside of 10 years—and conclude that GEICO is not digitizing the soul of their business. GEICO has attention and that attention is creating revenue, but the attention doesn't stick. Consumers aren't making an emotional attachment to the cost savings and humorous cartoon advertising on which GEICO drives new business.

If you're a small to mid-size insurance agency competing against GEICO, your only offensive strategy is to connect with consumers on a deeper level. This is the same for start-ups searching for the gap in the market that their larger, more established competitors don't currently fill. You can sit on the sideline pushing price and product, or you can look deep inside your organization to share the "Why."

A company that sits on the sideline is just another commodity. GEICO is very good at selling a commodity, but as The Hanover Insurance Group's study shows, consumers have made little to no emotional connection to the brand.

Today's Connected Generation consumer wants more out of their product and service providers. These consumers want to know who you are and how your products or service benefits them. The brands that are winning the battle for attention are going a step further and creating an experience around their brand that consumers can connect to on a deeper level and use as a piece of self-expression.

We live in a world of options, and our decision to digitize the soul of our business can either make us "*The* Choice"—or just another choice in the sea of vendors and commodity pushers.

High school football taught me a very important lesson: Whether you

34

succeed or fail in your effort, the pain of impact is always substantially less when *you* deliver the blow. Likewise, the pain of failure is less for those who instigate the action.

Fail as a result of action. Learn, adjust, repeat. This is how you become a better football player. It is also how you succeed in marketing your business in the digital world.

It's time to step out into the world and deliver your blow. **Bring the fight to your competition by telling your story, and the story of those you serve in the digital world.** Digitize the soul of your business, for our battle as marketers and business owners isn't over lines on a football field, but the hearts and minds of our respective consumers.

» EXERCISE:

Create accountability partnerships within your organization to ensure the opportunities found in Step 3 are acted upon here in Step 4. I know, from presenting across the United States for more than three years on digital marketing, that the vast majority of people reading this book won't act on it. Inaction is a sad truth.

35

No action, no results. The best way to ensure action is to be accountable to someone else. Traditionally, we're accountable to a manager or higher-up within an organization, the boss or a board. But according to Mike Thaman, CEO of Owens Corning, there is a huge difference between "holding someone accountable," which has mainly negative and punitive connotations, and "creating accountability in others," which is about being vested in the performance success of others.

Whether you use accountability systems or not, the simple truth is that you have to do the work of creating the content that will spread your message to the Product Market Fit audience.

The five stages of digitizing the soul of your business could possibly be the most important lessons you take away from this book. Car buyers will max their budgets for a Mercedes instead of a more affordable Infiniti, *if* they feel connected and activated.

The companies that create a content marketing culture will embrace small setbacks, solicit audience feedback, adapt their messages and re-implement on the fly. Such companies will be the winners in Content Warfare.

Everyone else will be chasing the next set of marketing tactics while complaining about the ROI (Return on Investment).

Currency of the Internet

I know what you're thinking. You can't make your mortgage payment with attention.

But maybe you can.

Attention is the currency of the Internet.

There is no denying that fact. Every day, there are millions of pieces of content created by individuals and brands, seeking the attention of Connected Generation consumers.

Without attention, your message doesn't spread, potential customers pass you by, and your business doesn't grow.

You know this. I know this. We all know this.

So we do things to attract attention. We write articles on trending topics that don't relate to our business. We write more. We pay for ads. We regurgitate the same tired information with a new catchy headline. We whore ourselves out to every new strategy and tactic on every new social network *(and established social networks)* where anyone with half a brain can post on.

Attention without trust holds no value.

To win the battle for attention online, the audience we serve must trust the work we do.

When I first started my work online, marketing myself as the Albany Insurance Professional, I was consuming every piece of content I could possibly find. This was the 2008-2009 timeframe. Looking back, I was very lucky, because the thought-leaders I came in contact with during this time played a major role in shaping my beliefs about digital marketing.

One such thought-leader was Chris Brogan, co-author of the bestselling book *Trust Agents*. At this time, he was producing a video series titled, "Overnight Success." In this video series, Brogan took raw footage shots with his smartphone and gave commentary on the drudgery involved in being an "overnight success." Whether it was waking up at 3 a.m. to catch a flight to speak at an event, or dealing with the harsh realities of limited family time, Brogan shared the work it takes to spread a message you believe in.

I've tried to say this to Chris in person, but I don't know if he'll never truly understand what a meaningful impact his *Overnight Success* video series had on the trajectory of my career. Partially, I responded to its inside look at the work it takes to be a success. But what hit me most profoundly was the power of authenticity, honesty and transparency. Chris Brogan had been doing the same work for almost ten years when his message finally hit the mainstream marketing consciousness. He wasn't an Overnight Success: he was a worker, a journeyman and a believer.

There would have been easier ways for Brogan to attract attention than videoing himself at these oddball times, talking into technology that today we'd consider antiquated and cumbersome. But the point of the video series wasn't just attention: it was trust.

38 **The "attention" part is easy. It's the trust part that takes time.**
This is why get-rich-quick schemes are only as profitable as the next get-rich-quick scheme. Attention is fleeting and whimsical. But trust makes you more than just today's special flavor of ice cream.

And here's the part most marketers miss: to those with trust, attention seems almost effortless. These individuals could walk on stage, fart into the microphone and the audience would clap and cheer and line up afterwards to express its gratitude . . .

. . . because of trust.

Trust gives attention value.

Attention does not equal trust.

Understanding this distinction is the key to sustainable success in the digital world.

Which means more attention isn't the goal.

More trust is. Which only further emphasizes the need to focus on the accumulation of True Fans.

The Golden Age of Attention

Let's now dispel the myth of decreasing attention spans.

In 2012, a Pew Research Center study concluded that, "The current generation of internet consumers lives in a world of 'instant gratification and quick fixes' which leads to a 'loss of patience and a lack of deep thinking.' "

Marketing gurus, rock stars and ninjas have used this research and similar studies to claim that long-form content marketing is dead. "How can you be successful creating long-form content when Internet consumers have the attention span of a gnat?" they'll ask. All the while, they're pushing their next Twitter, Facebook or Instagram marketing course, which normally costs $897, but if you buy it in the next ten minutes and use the double secret promo code, it's only $97.

Twitter, Facebook and Instagram are great. I'm all about visual storytelling and the viral power of a well-timed, high-quality image or quote on social media. But I'm not buying that attention spans are getting shorter, or that long-form content marketing is dead.

40

I think there are a lot of marketers who would love for you to believe this, because it makes digital marketing seem easier. Just look at the words: "short-form" seems easier than "long-form." But the truth is, it's all nonsense.

How can I say this?

The average viewer of my podcast, Content Warfare on Content Warfare TV, listens for over 21 minutes.

21 minutes . . . does that show a decrease in attention spans?

How about more than 76 million people watching the three minute and twenty nine second First Kiss video that went viral?

To those who say, "It's all about micro-content," I say I'm not so sure.

How about this: According to the New York *Times*, 33 articles of more than

4,000 words originated on the front page in 2012. That's up—a lot—from 16 the previous year; 21 in 2010; and 23 in 2009.

Why would the NY *Times* be willing to continually increase the amount of long-form content if their readers weren't interested? They wouldn't: happy readers are the NY *Times*' business. Happy readers mean more pageviews, which, in turn, means more ad revenue.

We're currently living through the Golden Age of Attention.

Web viewers are more willing than ever to give their attention to content creators . . . with just one caveat.

Your content has to be good. Screw that . . .your content has to kick ass. It has to add value to viewers' lives, and not just once. One-hit wonders won't survive.

I believe these statistics prove a maturation in Internet content consumers.

And by maturation, I mean that content consumers are willing to discriminate against shallow, valueless content. Today's mature, Connected Generation consumer is less likely to chase headlines or tolerate poor web design. The Connected Generation is unwilling to give content one more extra millisecond than it deserves.

41

So here's my advice: a storm is coming. Gurus, rock stars, and ninjas are gearing up for the crushing message of "*Micro-content.*" I believe that micro-content is important, and it helps to continually drip out your message, but NEVER give up on long-form content marketing and rich media content marketing.

→ Stay true to the course.

Long-form content marketing is the past, present and future of growing your business online.

The Perfect Online Audience

In pursuit of the perfect online audience, my mind tends to travel two different paths: that of the artist and of the marketer.

The Artist would tell you to always be true to yourself. Be unique, do what you love, say what you want, the way you want to say it . . .
. . . and the audience that relates to your content, ideas and style will spread your message.

The Marketer would tell you to tailor your message to the specific audience you wish to attract. Do market research, keyword research and A/B testing
. . .
. . . and your calculated message will attract the audience searching for solutions to the calculated problem your message solves.

Both theories seem sound, yet neither will attract the perfect online audience.

42   The artist's audience wants to experience a message. They want to soak it in and make it a new piece of who they are. The artist's audience seeks brands to use as self-expression. The artist's audience feels fulfilled sharing your message with friends, as sharing your art implies their own creativity and genius.

The marketer's audience is interested in the cold, hard solution. They derive value from the quality of product they're consuming. The relationship is a transaction, and if quality diminishes, they're moving on.

To find our perfect audience, we must capture the consumers who are also True Fans. The problem in finding your perfect online audience is that it takes work, and a crystal clear understanding of who your True Fans are.

Finding your perfect audience has nothing to do with the audience.

We must create an accurate, engaging, concise value statement, and then shake out everyone who doesn't fit.

What about all the people who sign up for your email list who will never buy from you?

Those people are The Artist's audience.

What about those people who buy from you, but don't subscribe to your email list and refuse to connect with you on social media?

These people are The Marketer's audience.

Your perfect online audience doesn't have to be your entire audience, but they should be the only portion of your audience that you strive to fulfill with every piece of content, every product, every action to you take online.

Here's a 6 step process for finding your perfect online audience:

1. *Define exactly who you help.*
This should be one to three sentences (the shorter the better) outlining, NOT who you are or who you want to help, but who you *do* help.

2. *Search out your perfect audience*   43
Where do the people or businesses you help hang out? Go there. Be present. Be useful. . . and DON'T sell.

3. *Listen to what your perfect online audience wants*
What your True Fans want isn't always what they need. But if you don't give them what they want *first*, you'll never have the opportunity to show them what they need.

4. *Address your perfect online audience with specific lead capture pages {filter #1}[Is the 'filter' a picture or a graph?]*
Your lead capture pages (landing pages) should address one specific group of people, your True Fans. Use the unique language and terminology you learned by listening. **WARNING:** *Do not build your lead capture pages as "Catch all" forms; these should each be specific to the type of person you want to attract and the action you want that person to take.*

5. *Build an email auto-responder with messaging to filter out unqualified leads {filter #2}*
This email autoresponder sequence is NOT meant to be a sleazy sales

funnel, blasting marketing messages into as many email inboxes as possible. Rather, these messages can explain how True Fans benefit from your content and, potentially, your products. Encourage uninterested parties to unsubscribe.

6. *Begin to deliver free value consistently*
Only now do you begin to explain how your products and services can help solve your True Fans' problems through masterfully written copy that both helps your audience and sells them at the same time.

We don't need a large audience. We just need the right audience.

Build Your Community First

When I first started creating content online, it was terrible.

The writing was terrible.

The formatting was terrible.

My keyword research was terrible.

My technical SEO and content marketing strategies were terrible.

None of these were even the worst part. The actual content itself was terrible. Everything I spewed out felt unoriginal and uninspired, *the antithesis of awesome.*

This is why, over the years, I've been so appreciative of the people who've followed my work since the early days. It was rough back then, but these True Fans saw something in me and stuck around. We got to know each better, connected on various social media platforms and, with some, I've been so lucky as to have met IRL (in real life).

45

We built our community of Content Warriors one at a time.
Therein lies a lesson.

The longevity of a brand online rests upon the passion and loyalty of the community supporting it. Community-building is a Day One activity. For most of us, the content we create is NOT awesome at the beginning. Our vision may be awesome. Our product may be awesome. Our people may be awesome. But when we first start on the path of content marketing, the content we create is most likely not going to be awesome, and we need to be OK with that.

Creating truly awesome, valuable content takes practice, dedication and time. We have to put in the work, experience the failures, and strengthen our online voices.

There is no more powerful incubator of valuable content than our community of True Fans.

Because it's hard to grow in a vacuum.

Think of your content as a rose bush and your community as the environment surrounding it. A vibrant community of passionate, motivated individuals provides support, guidance, feedback and reach to your message. These are the soil, water, nutrients and air your rose bush needs to grow the deep roots and strong stem necessary to support the beautiful flower that will eventually blossom.

It's impossible for your rose bush to blossom without the support of its environment.

Our community supports us through the tough times, and amplifies our success in the good times.

I have built multiple communities:

1. Google Plus is my primary social network and my fastest-growing community.

2. The Content Warfare Podcast listeners are probably my most engaged and loyal community.

3. The Content Warfare Newsletter readers are my longest-running community, with the first subscribers having opted in over two years ago.

4. and I just started building a community on YouTube, where I want to deliver content the way my audience has asked for it.

Each community is its own unique space. I provide value to each community by considering its own unique qualities, and each community plays its own unique role in supporting the Content Warfare brand.

If I waited till I was awesome at creating YouTube videos before I started building a community on YouTube, there would be no one there to spread my awesome video when I decided to hit publish. Additionally, these early community members provide feedback and insight into how I can improve my content creation more rapidly.

That's the key thought in this discussion as we move out of this first section on How to Find Your Audience into the next, more tactical section:

Telling Your Story.

If you want your content to spread, then you must build your communities from the start. Content doesn't spread because you want it to. People who enjoy your content and/or believe in the message spread your content.

Your success or failure online depends on the True Fans your brand accumulates. These individuals are the bedrock of your community. The reach of your content is limited only by the size of your community of True Fans.

Tactics are easy. It's the consistently creating value part that's hard.

Give me two days and I can teach you every vital tactic for marketing your business online. Two days, and you'll be a rock star of digital marketing, a master of social media. You'll know every trick, tactic and best practice as if you were born with the knowledge. But if you can't conceptualize the value you add to the consumers you serve—and effectively convey it to them—you're certain to fail.

47

Every piece of content we create, whether for a blog, social media or email marketing, should be created with the intention of building community, and ultimately generating revenue. When done correctly, the results are undeniable (as I shared in my 100 Questions Answered campaign).

If you consistently create content with the purpose of adding immense value to the personal and professional lives of the community members you serve, revenue generation is the result.

So the question really is, "*How do we add immense value?*"

There was a day when the value we provided to our clients was the expertise we accumulated through experience, mentorship, training and networking with colleagues. Every business operates in a complex yet delicate ecosystem, easily confused and contaminated with misconceptions.

Before the Internet, we stood as masters in our areas of expertise, as gatekeepers to that knowledge. If our customers had a question, concern or problem, they needed us to find the solution. Unfortunately, that value proposition no longer exists.

We are no longer the gatekeepers of our expertise. The Internet has reversed the flow of value, and consumers can now find everything they need to know on the Internet. To survive, we must adapt.

The critical value we provide consumers is NOT our product knowledge, but rather our experience and guidance throughout the buying process and after the sale.

Consumers of the Connected Generation want to know everything there is to know about a product or service before they purchase. By embracing digital and social media marketing, our business will become both the information source, and the guide for these connected consumers.

If we do not engage, the information void will be filled by those who are willing to engage. To quote Michael J. Fox's character in *The American President:* "People want leadership, Mr. President, and in the absence of genuine leadership, they'll listen to anyone who steps up to the microphone."

Never has there been a time in history when it was so quick, easy and inexpensive to deliver a message to consumers. Content marketing is a *gift*. It levels the playing field. With amplifiers like blogs, social media, email marketing and customer relationship management tools, we can take back the airways.

So what am I asking you to do? *Create content with reckless abandon.* Create content that tells your story over and over again, till every single client knows exactly who you are, why you're in business, and the value you provide.

Simon Sinek, the author of *Start With Why*, said in his now famous TED Talk, "The Golden Circle": "People don't buy what you do, they buy why you do it." It's the "*Why*" of what we do that spreads our message.

It's the "Why" of what we do that creates True Fans of our brand.

Our task now is refocusing our efforts from "*What*" to "*Why*," because "*Why*" makes the phone ring.

We are no longer the gatekeepers of our expertise. We didn't choose for this transformation to happen, but it's happened nonetheless. Now it's time for everyone, no matter who you are—from the one-person clothing shop to the locally-sourced farm stand to the regional insurance agency—to **tell your story of** *"Why."*

Using the communication mediums of today, we can deliver our value-driven marketing messages to the Connected Generation, create communities of True Fans, and ensure the success of our businesses in the digital marketplace.

« Case Study »

"Be unique. You have to be unique or you're just going to be like everybody else. Insurance can be so bland and websites can be so boring that if you don't stand out, you're not really going to catch anybody's attention. " ~ Denny Christner, InsureMyFoodTruck.com   49

To this point in the book you've heard a lot about my own work and what I've done to harness the power of content marketing and storytelling, and ultimately grow whatever business I was working for at the time.

Now I want to introduce a new case study, and tell the story of Denny Christner and InsureMyFoodTruck.com. The following is a conversation/case study between Denny and myself discussing the genesis of InsureMyFoodTruck.com and how he leveraged content marketing and social media to win the battle for attention in his niche.

At first glance, BayRisk Insurance Brokers, Inc, is your standard hardworking, service-based independent insurance agency, similar to the 22,000 other independent insurance agencies located throughout the U.S. They sell similar products, in similar ways, to similar clients. By all accounts BayRisk Insurance is a well-run, yet relatively standard insurance agency.

That is, they were, until Denny Christner, one of three principals at the agency, came upon a gourmet Food Truck in downtown San Francisco, CA. A "foodie" at heart, Denny started visiting the gourmet food trucks that line the streets of San Francisco simply because he enjoyed the meals they created.

As insurance agents happen to do, (it actually might be part of their DNA), Denny started asking food truck owners about their insurance. Quickly, Denny realized that food trucks are not necessarily an easy type of insurance to write—or, rather, that's what most of his competitors believed.

After making phone calls to a few different insurance carriers, Denny not only found an insurance carrier with the appetite to write food truck insurance, but saw immense opportunity in an incredibly un-served market.

"We had a couple [food trucks] on the books, [but] I didn't really understand the [food truck] industry until actually going to an event. I thought, 'Oh, okay. This is what it's really all about,' and [I] talked to those couple clients I had and said, 'What do you guys need?' and 'How is this industry changing?' I got ideas from my clients and then pitched the brand to my partners before I actually had a product."

Like most of Denny's insurance agent competition, his partners didn't at first see opportunity in the food truck industry like Denny did. This is a big reason many content marketing campaigns never get off the ground: It's incredibly difficult to get buy-in from management, especially in an industry like insurance (and there are many others) where successful content marketing case studies are few and far between.

"Yeah. I did have to sell my partners on it because it's an expense to start a niche without an existing book. There're advertising dollars, there's website billing, there's the cost of time. Everything involved in starting a niche is thousands of dollars. It's a lot of work and it's a lot of time."

Work. Time. At this point, you're probably sick of hearing me preach the hard work and time that is required to win the battle for attention. There is a reason I sound like a broken record. For all the tactics and strategies that exist for marketing your business and brand online, **there is always**

50

one constant among the winners: hard work and the persistence to put in the time.

The rub, however, is that regardless of how much time you're willing to put in or how hard you're willing work, opportunity has to exist in order for your content marketing efforts to be worth that time and hard work.

"You have to do the big picture thing," Denny said. "It has to make sense . . . as far as the world of your niche. Like, if I had wanted to go after something that was very small—if it didn't have the opportunity, didn't have the premium (and therefore revenue) behind it—it just wouldn't make sense. But when I explained [to my partners] that this industry is booming and there are 10,000 food trucks in California alone— if we write ten percent of that business and we expand that nationally, we're looking at X amount of premium; X amount of revenue."

Taking his partners to events that showcased the food truck industry helped, too.
"That kind of was the tipping point," said Denny, "when the local organizers opened an event in our small . . . town of Alameda, and they came to that event and understood, 'Whoa! There's an hour line for a food truck!' Like they had no idea until coming to an event how popular it was." 51

Unfortunately, opportunity alone doesn't guarantee success online. Denny recognized the opportunity that food trucks presented to his business and was successful in getting buy-in from other stakeholders in his business. The rocket was on the launch pad, fueled and ready for liftoff. But that was only half the battle.

There was still a lot more work that had to be done to get his content marketing rocket ship into space.

"I started hitting the blog up hard in the beginning," said Denny. "I was blogging three, maybe four times a week, and I really developed the content early, before I actually I had clients. I was doing the research, and advocating for food trucks, and talking to industry leaders and writing content, all about food trucks before I even had a great product to offer them.

"Our SEO jumped really quick and I think we started ranking [for relevant keyword terms] . . . either three or four, probably within four months of writing content pretty heavy," he said.

But as we have already discussed, we can't just blog to blog, there must be a method. Think back to my 100 Insurance Questions Answered campaign: the crux of the success of that campaign was using the exact words my clients used.

Denny got content ideas from "talking to the clients and going to the events and figuring out what kind of coverage was important to them and writing about the loss of business income, equipment breakdown, the spoilage, things that are triggers for them . . . which a lot of companies weren't offering. We were able to partner with the MGA (Insurance carrier representative) that had a program to offer those coverages that were of interest to the prospective clients."

The blogging piece of the InsureMyFoodTruck.com story is hopefully very exciting. If an independent insurance agent (someone in a boring business) can find success harnessing the power of content marketing to a very specific, almost obscure niche like food trucks, then you can find success no matter what your business or industry.

52

Content marketing works . . . it's just work.

Though interesting and exciting, Denny and the InsureMyFoodTruck.com case study isn't necessary unique or special— yet. What makes this case study special isn't how Denny found the food truck market (which is what we've explained so far), but rather how and where he told his story.

"A big issue for this clientele (food trucks) is that they are very fast paced. They're very social orientated," Denny said. "I mean, social media . . . Twitter is where we started getting the most attention before we were ranking. I was getting phone calls [saying they found me] on Twitter; I was getting direct messages via Twitter for quotes.

"Some people . . . I never even emailed or talked to on the phone. It was just all Twitter conversations," Denny said. "I had to work fast for them. It's a fast industry, so if you're not responsive, they're already onto the next person who is willing to give them a quote. We try to turn quotes around same day or next day. "

The mistake too many businesses make when they first engage in content marketing? Believing that they can dictate where conversations happen. Though the insurance industry as a whole is incredibly guilty of this, they are not alone.

Just because it's most convenient for you to communicate in a certain way, does not mean that is also the most convenient way for your customers to communicate. Twenty years ago, this wasn't an issue. Technology did not provide the options it does today. Customers who wanted a certain product or service were forced to communicate using the method preferred by the provider.

The Internet has destroyed this business practice. Today consumers have the ability, using the Internet, to find the product or service provider who communicates in the exact method they prefer. As Denny did by taking to Twitter—a medium for which there was no precedent of success within the insurance industry—you must seek out and utilize the communication methods preferred by your audience or they will find someone who will. 53

But dictating communication medium isn't the only Old World business practice the Internet has destroyed. As mentioned in the section Finding Your Audience, the Internet (most notably Google) has also destroyed the generalist online. As Denny explains:

"I thought it was important to brand ourselves. What's BayRisk to somebody who is not in the Bay Area? Or . . . what does BayRisk really mean to a food truck? It doesn't really have any correlation."

But, Denny went on, "By branding 'Insure My Food Truck', not only is it clear what we do, but we're going to rank higher [in what] people . . . search for: 'How Do I Insure My Food Truck?'

Denny and his partners choose to brand their niche campaign completely separate from their BayRisk Insurance brand, despite BayRisk's decades-long existence. They knew the only way to stand out online was to create a brand that positioned their business as the expert in food truck insurance.

Food truck owners who go Google searching for a solution to their insurance needs aren't looking for an insurance agency who writes food trucks. They are searching for the expert in food truck insurance, someone who knows the business and unique set of insurance risks food truck owners face every day.

In 2012, no other insurance agency in the entire country had positioned themselves in this way: only InsureMyFoodTruck.com. For food truck owners, choosing to work with Denny and InsureMyFoodTruck.com was a no-brainer.

"We've now built a referral base where these guys all talk," Denny said in 2014. "They're parked next to each other for hours. They eat each other's food and they talk and say, 'My insurance is coming up and I pay $5,000 grand a year. It's ridiculous. Who do you use?' and that's how we get our referrals, pretty much. But the SEO, I would say, is the number one source of traffic to the site as far as new business because we're ranked . . . last time I checked, we're number one or number two, plus the next seven slots via Facebook, YouTube, whatever it is. We rank probably eight of the top 13 sites on page one of Google."

And what do food truck owners find when they get to InsureMyFoodTruck. com? An open and honest discussion on the food truck industry. The clearest representation of this is the inclusion of insurance policy pricing listed on the website, a practice almost unheard of outside the retail industry (and doubly unheard of in any service-based business such as insurance).

"There're a few reasons we included price on our website. One, the program we use doesn't vary on price all that much. It's safe to say . . . " Denny said, adding that big cities like New York or Boston would be much more expensive.

"But for the most part, the program rates don't differ all that much. We feel comfortable throwing a ball park [figure] out there. But the major reason is because these guys don't have a lot of time. They're just interested in finding a professional, making sure the price is reasonable, and getting it done."

By going to the site, Denny said, potential customers can see, "These guys are professional. Here's, basically, their ball park price, and here's their quote request form that takes me two minutes. All 1-2-3. Done."

Most businesses would look at the practice of sharing rates online as blasphemy. What if the competition sees our rates and undercuts our price? A legitimate, but narrow-sighted question. **Denny proves that understanding your audience and providing what they need, on their terms, wins attention every time.**

Through the hard work that Denny has put in at InsureMyFoodTruck.com, the food truck industry no longer views his business as simply a provider of a product they need, but rather a trusted resource.

"I get people in the insurance industry asking me, 'How do you do it? I want to do this,' for my niche and I'm happy to share what I did, but I think where people go wrong is that they're not willing to really devote all of their time on it.

"I was literally working like 18 hours a day for weeks, months to get this thing launched," Denny said. "It's so time-focused that a lot of people just aren't willing to give up their weekends and evenings to dedicate to a niche."

55

There it is, my friends:

"Where people go wrong is that they're not willing to really devote all of their time on it." Content marketing works—it's just work. It takes time, energy and effort to find your audience, tell your story and win the battle for attention online.

However, if you are willing to dedicate yourself and follow the process laid out in this book, eventually you will win and the opportunities that surface, forged from the compound growth of your effort every day, will make the juice well worth the squeeze.

Finishing our conversation, Denny left me with this quote, which perfectly summarizes the journey every marketer must make to win the battle for attention online:

"I think it's important for people to not expect overnight (monetary) success. It's easy to get burnout when it takes a long time to create a brand, content and everything that comes along with it, and not see quick bottom line results. My income stayed flat in 2012, even though that was the hardest year I ever worked. Now I still work my ass off, but the revenue machine is flowing mostly because of that first year of work."

Denny found his audience, told a story Food Truck owners wanted and needed to hear and, ultimately, through hard work and perseverance, won the battle for attention online. Now this niche market he has built is consistently the highest gross revenue producing segment of the BayRisk Insurance agency.

The Numbers

In 2012, when Denny began his work on the business that ultimately became InsureMyFoodTruck.com, BayRisk Insurance Brokers, Inc. was approximately a $2 million a year revenue business.

56 As Denny said above, at the end of 2012, the BayRisk bottom line was barely impacted by their work in the food truck industry. But by the end of 2013, InsureMyFoodTruck.com added 8 percent growth to the overall BayRisk operation. That's approximately $160,00 in revenue. *Content marketing works.*

When I talked to Denny in September of 2014, in the third quarter of his third year growing InsureMyFoodTruck.com, projected revenue growth to BayRisk from InsureMyFoodTruck.com was 17 percent year over year. That equates to approximately $365,000 in new business revenue.

→ **Content marketing works . . .It's just work.**

57

58

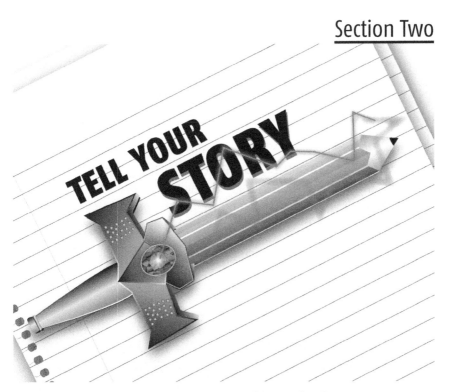

"What is the best type of content to create for my blog?"

This is, by far, the question I'm asked the most at presentations and interviews, by email and on social media.

My response is always the same:
Answer questions, openly and honestly, as best you can, as often as you can. This is the path to content marketing success.

That's it: answer questions. This is the most effective form of content marketing you can produce online. People visit the sites they visit for the reasons they visit them. Meaning, I don't go to Google to hangout, I go to Google+ or Facebook. When I go to Google Search, I have a problem or a question that I need solved. In this hypothetical scenario, if your company provides the solution to my problem, what better way to let Google know that you're the solution, than to answer the exact question I have?

Though Google's official mission statement doesn't say it, the core mission of its search engine is very simple: to match every problem with the best possible solution. This simple mission dictates every action Google has taken, every new product, every search algorithm update since Google Search was launched.

It's easy to get frustrated by the changes to Search. We spend so much time figuring out the rules just to have everything change again.

Let's forget about the algorithm for a minute and focus on nothing but providing the best possible user experience, and giving potential customers the most valuable solutions to every problem they could possibly have. If we do this, the latest change to Google or our favorite social network doesn't matter.

If your content is focused on solutions, then Google is always going to try and match the consumers with the corresponding problem to you. Slightly oversimplified, but true.

The power of answering questions in your content marketing isn't breaking news by any means. If anything, it's one of the foundational principles of content marketing. A pillar upon which all great content marketing tactics and strategy have been built.

Just a year ago, in 2013, a good friend of mine, Marcus Sheridan, known to some as "The Pool-guy" and others "The Sales Lion," was featured in an article in the New York *Times*. The story focused on Sheridan's work using content marketing to resurrect his dying fiberglass pool company, River Pools and Spas. The title of that article? "A Revolutionary Marketing Strategy: Answer Customers' Questions."

Look at that title, "A Revolutionary Marketing Strategy: Answer Customer' Questions." I'd like to ruminate on the word "revolutionary" for a second. Content marketing as a practice has been around for a hundred years. At the turn of 20th century John Deere Tractor created their own farming magazine, The Furrow and Ford Motors bought a local newspaper, The Dearborn Independent, to report on their respective company happenings. Another popular early example of content marketing was Guinness Breweries publishing the Guinness Book of World Records in 1955.

The throughout the history of content marketing, smart companies and marketers have been answering client questions as a way to provide for their current and potential customers. But in 2013, The New York *Times* declared Marcus's strategy of answering client questions "revolutionary."

He laughs about it today and, to those of us who live and breathe this work, it is kinda funny when you think about such a simple concept being anything other than standard practice.

Maybe that's why I decided to write a book about content marketing, and spend so much time inside that book talking about a principle that's been around since the very beginning of content marketing existence.

Actually, there are two reasons I wrote this book:

» First, content marketing is only "Old-hat" to experienced online marketers, as proved in the story about Marcus Sheridan. To the vast majority of mid- to small-sized businesses out there, content marketing as legitimate, revenue-driving business is still very new.

» Second, looking out over the landscape of content that is being created everyday online, I'm saddened by how often we stray from the straight-forward effort of answering customer questions. Experienced online marketers forego answering client questions in exchange for seemingly-sexier tactics and tricks, while most businesses are simply ignorant of the strategy's power.

What's the best type of content?

Well, I guess that depends—unless your goal is attracting targeted consumers, actively searching for a solution to their problem. Then the answer is simple: *answer customer questions.*

→ What questions can you start answering today?

Expertise Alone Will Not Grow Your Business

Expertise is the barrier to entry, not the catalyst for success.

Not knowing this is a huge mistake made by marketers and business owners alike when they first take their business online or start an online business. Expertise is not a guarantee of success, and only in rare cases is expertise even a differentiating characteristic.

Mark Traphagen, Senior Vice President of Online Marketing at Stone Temple Consulting, is one of (if not THE) most knowledgeable non-Google employees, helping marketers and business owners tap into the power of the Google+ platform. His expertise is unquestionable and rivaled by few in the world, but his expertise is only a small piece of how he's grown his personal brand so rapidly. In Mark's case, his Google+ follower count rose from just under 10,000 to over 50,000 in a matter of months (continuing upward to more than 95,000).

Don't get me wrong, I'm not using social media follower count as an exact indicator of success or influence. I would never recommend considering social media follower count as a KPI (key performance indicator) for your business.

However, social media follower counts (and, more importantly, social media view counts) can be incredibly valuable top-of-funnel metrics. In Mark's case, he's had more than 25,000,000 views of his content on Google+ alone.

Why am I sharing these numbers with you?

Because Mark is a master networker and relationship builder. He's willing to give now to get later, and he works his ass off forging new relationships with the most established SEO and content marketing experts, as well as with Google's own employees. He even takes the time to reach out to other content creators (such as myself) and help them spread their messages when he can.

Mark's expertise in Google+, SEO, and personal branding is his ticket in the door. But what gets him on stage is the network of relationships he's built over time. He's telling his story and building his audience, accumulating one True Fan at a time.

This example holds true outside of the virtual world as well. Take any traditional sales organization and ask their highest performing producer, "What makes people buy?"

None of them—none—will say, "Expertise." Expertise is a barrier for entry.

I know this from my work as an insurance agent. Sure, I got appointments because I knew insurance, but sales came as a result of the relationship built with the prospect, and how tightly intertwined our personal networks were. If we shared many overlapping connections, then my relationship-building work was much easier than if we shared few connections or none at all.

This phenomena transcends every industry, everywhere in the world, at any time in human history.

63

Why, then, would it not translate to the virtual world?

The fact is, relationship-building is just as, if not more, important to a virtual business than to a brick-and-mortar. We can't win the battle for attention by ourselves. No matter how smart you are, no matter how well you know a topic, no matter how much research you do or how often you post your expertise to a blog or social media or through a podcast, we need friends to spread our message. True Fans.

The most well-known in every industry get this. We've all heard the saying, "It's not what you know, it's who you know." Take that to the tenth power in the digital world. If you don't have True Fans, you're simply tweeting to yourself.

As we begin to understand how to tell our story online, always keep your True Fans in mind.

Most readers, viewers and listeners of your content are not going to Tweet out your latest post just because you published it. There are two reasons why members of your audience would be willing to share your content with their networks:

1. You've added so much value to their lives and/or businesses, they feel obligated to share your content.

2. Your content is so valuable and held in such regard that their sharing of your article makes them look better to *their* audiences.

That's it. Those are the two reasons.

» Guilt Marketing

Some content creators will try and guilt their audience into sharing their content by asking for shares over and over again, and explaining how important sharing is to the creator's success.

There is no doubt that if you ask enough people enough times to share your content (and you've made the process easy enough), you will get some shares. Unfortunately, this brute force mention of attracting attention is unsustainable. This is a selfish form of marketing and, as we discussed in the previous section of this book, it's not a strategy for building a stable of True Fans.

So how do we make content sharing a sustainable, renewable and profitable process, without completely alienating our audience by browbeating them for shares every time they visit?

Give without expectation of reciprocation. Help as many people as possible (while sustaining your business) without regard for reciprocation or monetary reimbursement.

Become the resource. Always be adding value to your True Fans' lives and/or business.

Show up. Dedicate yourself to a schedule and stick to it.

If you give without always asking in return, become the resource your True Fans need, and show up when you say you will, then your audience will share without you asking. This type of work will create a moral obligation

64

to share within your audience, as you'll have become more than just a website they visit, but a part of who they are.

This is the power of telling your story online:

The creation, over time, of a digital army of True Fans, who believe that sharing your message is as important to their own success as it is to yours.

They'll share without regard for what you're actually publishing; sharing your content will just become part of their routine (See every Internet marketer and the number of Seth Godin posts they've shared to their Twitter feed).

Is telling your story online easy? No. It's hard as hell.

But it's also incredibly simple . . . and your expertise plays only a small role. We're building relationships one audience member at time by giving first, and by always delivering value.

It works in the offline world, and it certainly works online.

65

Telling Your Story is Just a Tool

Why do we need to "Tell a story" to win the battle for attention online? I can't tell you how many times I've been asked this question. When I use the word "story" in blog posts and podcast, presentations and interviews, some people envision J.R.R. Tolkien, George R.R. Martin or William Gibson, storytellers who lock themselves in cabins in the woods and create imaginary worlds out of thin air.

This is not what I mean by story.

Your business story is the story that is going to attract True Fans— who will, in turn, help you attract the attention necessary to build an audience that will grow your business. Your business story is actually the intersection of three concentric circles of content:

Your company. Your clients. Your community.

The purpose of creating content inside these three circles is that each adds a necessary component to the relationship you're trying to build with potential audience members.

Relationships with human beings—living, breathing, emotional human beings who, at the end of the day, really just want to trust the organizations from which they purchase the products and services necessary to live the life they want to live.

That's why people buy from us, isn't it? They want to live better lives. They want to feel good. They want to feel happy: secure, excited, safe, powerful, successful. People buy from us because of the way our product or service makes them *feel about themselves.*

Telling our story helps potential customers better understand how our products and services will make them feel about themselves.

How does your product make your clients feel? I bet you don't know—or at least would have to guess if asked directly.

66 How does the way you sell your product or service make your clients feel about themselves? Have you even thought about that before? How we describe our product plays a huge role in who buys it.

Right now, you're telling a story about your business. But you may not realize it—which ultimately means you're not in control of that story.

The world is being commoditized. There is little debate to that fact. Big brands try harder and harder to produce more with less. This exercise forces the creation of mechanical systems; more mechanical systems create less differentiation; less differentiation creates more commoditization. Eventually, we find ourselves producing the same product as our competition . . . so we turn to the marketing and public relations and advertising departments and task *them* with making our product different.

But consumers are smart. The Internet has taken away Oz's curtain. In today's world, marketing, PR and advertising CAN'T differentiate you.

I know that might sound weird inside a book about content marketing. But we have to get this clear before we move forward. The marketing you're going to learn inside this book will help you grow your business, there is no doubt about that. But this strategy can't make your business unique. It can only help you highlight, distribute, and build communities around the aspects which make your business unique and awesome.

Does that make sense? It's vital that you understand this concept before we get into the nuts and bolts of telling your story. The story doesn't make your business unique. The mashup of you, your employees, your clients and the community your serve make your business unique. Telling the story of that uniqueness is just a marketing process.

Basically what I'm saying is, don't make up shit that isn't true because you're trying to make your business seem cool.

I cut my teeth on marketing in the insurance industry, a family-owned and -operated independent insurance agency. There are over 36,000 independent insurance agencies in the United States; the Northeast U.S. (the area of the country our agency is located in) has by far the densest population of independent insurance agencies in the country. From the sidewalk of our agency, I can see three other independent insurance agencies.

That's not including the State Farm, All State and Nationwide insurance offices (considered captive agencies) I can also see. And it doesn't include the GEICO, esurance and other direct writers selling insurance in the online space.

My point here is: most consumers do not understand the differences among their many options. Yes, the marketing is catchy and funny. . . but at the end of the day, what's the *difference*? Does it really matter where you buy your auto insurance?

If you try to differentiate yourself through marketing, there is no difference. Consumers are going to be attracted to the latest discount or funny commercial. There is no brand loyalty, no true attention paid to what a company stands for, or what the product really does. Insurance companies trying to differentiate themselves through marketing have commoditized the auto insurance market to a generation of consumers.

Now take my small, fifteen person independent agency. How are we supposed to differentiate ourselves through marketing? We can't compete with Geico. But the reality is, we *have* to compete with them, or our business won't be profitable.

We don't differentiate through marketing.

We use marketing to find and attract our True Fans. Those insurance consumers who share the same values and ideals for protecting their families and assets that we believe in as an insurance provider.

How we express those values and ideals lies in how we tell our story. Our story expresses who we are and who we're looking to attract.

In the scalable business world, most small businesses will lose trying to market ease of business and price. They lose every single time. That is a big business game, and most Big Businesses are damn good at it.

For my family's insurance agency, ease of business and price weren't our value proposition; they weren't our story. We sold *trust*: trust in service, trust in support, trust in accountability. I told our story over and over again to build that trust. Not to notify people of our latest discount . We tell the story of who we are or we will lose.

→ It's time to tell your story.

3 C's of Storytelling

Does the idea of "storytelling" petrify you, freezing your content marketing efforts?

Storytelling is one of 2014's hottest marketing buzzwords, according to Hubspot. Each new article on storytelling—heralding the work of corporate brands such as Apple and Disney, alongside personal brands such as Amanda Palmer—gave clear examples of the impact of storytelling.

"Content is dead. Long live storytelling," writes Jon Hamm in a recent article in Adweek.

Though fatalistic, I would agree, in so much as storytelling done right is a powerful form of content, and the brands who tell the right stories win.

On the surface, the concept of storytelling as a way to build brand loyalty and attract a targeted audience makes perfect sense. Create a story which resonates with a specific segment of the market, evoke positive emotion (or whatever type of emotion attracts your True Fans) and draw their attention to your brand.

69

Sounds simple enough . . . or does it?

Most businesses do not view themselves as storytellers—because they're not.

They're manufacturers, lawyers, accountants, builders, etc., and storytelling is the farthest thing from why they got into business in the first place.

The natural pushback from professionals who've read/heard/seen marketing agencies talking about storytelling usually comes in some variety of the protests below:

> » Who in my organization is supposed to tell stories?
>
> » How do stories convert into revenue?
>
> » My business doesn't have any interesting stories to tell.

Legitimate concerns for sure, and certainly cause for someone in a decision-making position to question the practice of storytelling in their corporate content marketing activities. When considering storytelling as a branding, community-building and/or revenue-generating tool, it's natural to dismiss the practice for its lack of clear ROI (return on investment).

We must think of storytelling in business as less Steven Spielberg and more iPhone home movie. Successful business storytelling removes the "Epic" associations, boiling the activity down to its purest form:
Conveying ideas through words and images with the goal of educating, entertaining and/or inspiring an audience.

Storytelling is just another term for good content marketing.
In just a moment, we'll use Apple's "Your Verse" commercial as a frame of reference for our discussion.

» 3 Cs of Storytelling in Business

70   There are 3 parts to business storytelling: **Company, Client, Community.**

Content created from the 3 Cs of storytelling in business form the narrative of our corporate story. Some pieces of content will focus on just your company, others just client or community. Others yet will encompass two or even three of Cs.

Apple's "Your Verse" commercial, an advertisement for the iPad Air tablet, is a well-done example of a short, lightly-produced piece of content which hits on all 3 Cs of storytelling in business.

1. Company

Let's start with what storytelling for your company is NOT. It's not a list of your products and services, industry awards or your latest sales pitch.

Tell the stories of the people who make up your company.

> » Where they've been,

> » Where they're going,

» What they do when they're not doing what your company does.

If you want to talk about your products, don't just tell people about them, show those products out in the world, doing what they do. This is what I love about the "Your Verse" commercial. Apple doesn't once mention the iPad Air tablet. However, you see the tablet in the video, in action almost a dozen times.

Don't tell your audience what your product or service does: show them.

2. Client

Some will call this, "Keeping up with the Joneses." But the truth is, we're wired to run with the pack. The social validation of seeing individuals we associate ourselves with using the same product makes us feel safe in our purchase.

People want to buy the things and use the services that people like them buy and use.

In the "Your Verse" video, Apple doesn't mention the specific types of people who would benefit from the iPad Air tablet. Instead, they put their would-be customers on display, filming them as they embark upon their creative endeavors using the iPad Air.

This commercial is appealing to society's creatives by showing them what is possible with a little bit of imagination—and an iPad Air tablet.

Highlight clients in your content to show your audience exactly who you help.

3. Community

Creating content about the community your business operates in, (be that physical or virtual), creates a sense that your business is one of "them". This is relatively easy for local businesses with a physical location, and more difficult for regional, national and virtual businesses.

Apple does this in the "Your Verse" commercial by showing behind-the-scenes shots. These seemingly-candid clips are meant to show creatives that Apple understands the work involved in creating their art. I would

71

argue these are the most important clips in the entire video.

Why are these behind-the-scenes clips so important?

Because only inside members of the creative community live behind the scenes. Apple is showing their potential clients that the iPad Air tablet is a tool accepted by the creative community.

Show your audience you're one of them.

Apple did all this in 91 seconds of spliced-together stock footage and a voice-over. When you break down the Apple "Your Verse" commercial into the 3 Cs, it becomes an incredibly powerful piece of storytelling.

You're telling me your business can't harness the power of storytelling?

Sure it can. We're not talking Pixar. Just sound content pulled from each of the 3 Cs of Storytelling in Business (and some reasonable professional editing.)

Storytelling as a Habit

Overcoming old habits is hard.

We assume that habits are part of who we are as people. We feel like that cup of coffee we have every morning, or the frigidity fingers we get when we're nervous, are just pieces of our personality.

These habits may feel like part of who we are, but our habits do not define us. If we let our habits define us, then we become a slave to them, and that closes down our world.

Letting our habits control our actions limits our availability to the possibility of success. Habits close doors, even good habits.

» The Morning Coffee

I love my coffee in the morning. I love it. I go to bed looking forward to the piping hot cup of coffee that is going to be waiting for me when I wake up.

73

One night as I was preparing the coffee for the following morning I accidentally dropped the pot into the kitchen sink and it subsequently shattered. All I could do was stare, horrified and heart-broken.

In a desperate attempt to reclaim my morning ritual I found a metal bowl and shoved it inside the coffee maker to catch the fresh brewed coffee. I went to bed, hoping to be satisfied when I woke up.

The habit, and my reluctance to break that habit, caused me to make a pretty stupid decision.

When I awoke, broken coffee pot half-forgotten, my morning coffee was lukewarm in the metal container and tasted funky. Not to mention that the coffee (which was not meant to be dispensed into a metal bowl) had splattered all over the countertop. It ruined my day. As crazy as that sounds, I ALLOWED coffee ruin my day.

» Habits Are a Choice

The way we form relationships on the Internet is habit. The time we spend (and where we spend that time) on the Internet is a habit. How we tell our story on the Internet is a habit.

In *The Flinch*, (a book published through Seth Godin's Domino Project), author Julien Smith explains how habits (such as flinching) hold us back from success.

Are you allowing a habit to hinder your success Online?

Do you waste valuable Internet time on Gossip or Sports sites that have no relevance to your business?

Do you respond to emails in short, incomplete sentences without much thought?

These are habits we need to break. Distracting, limiting habits can keep us from the success we desire—the success we can only achieve by doing the work of finding our audience and telling our story.

74 **Storytelling is a habit.**

Here are nine bad habits that keep us from telling our story online:

1. *No method for collecting story ideas*
Great content ideas are going to hit you at the most inopportune time. It's the nature of the universe. Don't fight the fact that your best ideas will happen in the shower or while driving. Instead, create methods to capture those ideas. Buy a writeable shower note pad (a real product!) and use the talk-to-text feature on your smartphone so you can keep two hands on the wheel while jotting down your idea.

2. *Too much time spent reading other people's content*
It's important to stay in-the-know on what's going on the world, but too much time spent reading other people's content greatly decreases your own time to create. The key is finding a balance. Schedule time for content consumption.

3. *No scheduled content creation time*

Building off of Number 2, the best way to ensure you have the time and attention to tell your story is to schedule blocks of time during the week to create. Schedule this time like you would an important meeting or sales call. Otherwise, it won't get done.

4. *Answering email immediately*
There is nothing more disrupting to your creative work than the need to check and respond to email every five minutes. Your brain doesn't simply pop in and out of creation mode. Stay focused and get the work done.

5. *Not creating content from smartphone*
For many professionals and business owners, lack of time is a major (and legitimate) reason for not telling their story online. Luckily, we have smartphones, which make content creation on-the-go easy and fast. Apps, such as Instagram, allow users to take, edit and share images with ease to social networks like Twitter and Facebook. Use apps like Wordswag or Over to add professional-style text to your images before sharing. All this can be done with just a few taps on your phone.

6. *Video games*
I'm not hating on gamers. If video games are your work or hobby, great. But they can easily suck hours out of your day. Many non-gamers use video games, such as Candy Crush or Angry Birds, to pass idle time. This time could be better spent brainstorming ideas of content, sharing content, or actually creating.

7. *Leaving smartphone push notifications on*
The only notification that pushes through my phone is my daily schedule. Turn everything else off. (See Number 4 on email.)

8. *Content curation*
Re-sharing other people's content into your stream can be a good way to tell your story online. But as a replacement for creating your own content, content curation becomes a very bad habit. Remember, the creators always win.

9. *Perfectionism*
Nothing you do online is ever going to be perfect. Stop planning, stop tweaking, stop editing, and hit publish. Waiting for your content to be

perfect before you hit publish is a first-class ticket to never achieving the success you desire.

» Our Success Is No Longer Dictated by Bad Habits

Let's initiate the change we desire in our lives. Let's agree to not let bad habits dictate our decisions. Coffee in the morning is great, but choose to drink it, don't let the need for coffee control your actions or your mood.

Easier said than done, I know. And I'm not so arrogant as to believe that a few words in a book, even a book so amazing as *Content Warfare*, can break you from giving in to bad habits. But if even, to a small extent, we're aware of what our bad content marketing habits are, we can begin to change those habits.

Business Storytelling

"Don't just write. Write about something. Do more than entertain. You're not a dancing monkey. You're a motherfucking storyteller, embrace that responsibility." ~ Chuck Wendig

Regardless of whether you write about insurance, information products, or industrial screw manufacturing, storytelling is what engages our audience, captures their attention, and ultimately turns them into customers and clients enamored by our brand, excited to come back over and over again.

Storytelling is a necessity.

Business storytelling.

Not Shakespeare, or *Game of Thrones*. In its content marketing context, 'storytelling' refers to the overall message delivered throughout the entire breadth of our content marketing efforts.

77

What does the content marketing body of work you've created to this point say about your business?

It's not one article that defines us. We are viewed by the sum of all the work we create.

The classic 'scrape and spin' articles just don't get the job done anymore. We need to be producing original content which, through business storytelling, brings in an audience, captures them, enamors them to us, and ultimately, turns them into paying customers and clients.

Audience first, always.

» The Customer Expectation Triangle of Death

Imagine a triangle. At one point is Price. At the second point is Quality. At the third and final point is Speed of Delivery. These points represent our customer expectations for every transaction they initiate.

Before 4G LTE, before social media, before smartphones, before widespread Wi-Fi, customers understood that that technology was such, product/service providers only deliver two sides of the triangle and their expectation reflected this understanding.

We could have high quality product and fast delivery, but our product or service was going to be expensive. We could have a cheap price and high quality, but delivery was going to be extremely slow.

Customers expected the companies they did business with to be able to deliver only two sides of the triangle. Before the Internet, if your business could deliver the third side of the triangle (high quality, cheap price *and* fast delivery), you were able to blow customer expectations away; word would spread and your business would dominate the market.

However, web 2.0, Wi-Fi, the Cloud—all these types of technology have changed customer expectations forever. Point of sale, database management, manufacturing, logistics, delivery, Amazon, Zappos, GEICO . . . Customers now expect a business, from a Fortune 500 to a corner bakery in small-town America, to deliver a high-quality product at a competitive price with immediate turnaround on their order.

The Customer Expectation Triangle of Death was given this moniker because, to today's modern marketplace consumer, if you're not providing all three sides of the Customer Expectation Triangle, your business is dead (or dying).

As matter of pure habit, during almost every one of my presentations, I'll turn to the audience ask, "Please raise your hand if service differentiates you from your competition."

Inevitably, ninety-plus percent of the audience will raise its hands.

"Look around," I'll say, "How can service differentiate your business if service differentiates every business?"

Great customer service doesn't differentiate your business. It's the barrier to entry. Great customer service is the expectation.

Great customer service, competitive rates, high quality products, ease and speed of business—we can no longer rest upon these common business features as differentiators. Our customers expect us to have great customer service, competitive rates, high quality products and fast delivery.

If you're not providing all three sides of the customer expectation triangle, potential customers will simply choose another provider.

The Internet, in addition to providing companies with the technology to provide all three sides of the Customer Expectation Triangle, has also provided customers with limitless options in who they do business with for just about every want or need they could possibly have.

If you're not providing all three sides of the customer expectation triangle, your business is already dying. You may not know it, you may not want to admit it, you may not feel it yet, but believe me, **Connected Generation consumers expect all three sides of the Customer Expectation Triangle.** Anything less is certain death.

» Customer Experience Trumps Expectation

You may be asking yourself, "What else is there? What else can I do, besides offer a great product at a competitive rate with fast delivery?"

As the three points of the Customer Expectation Triangle of Death are the now the barrier to entry into the modern marketplace, the differentiator becomes **Customer Experience.**

This, my friends, is where Content Warfare begins.

We don't win the battle for attention by creating and distributing content about our fast delivery, the features of our great product, or the speed and ease of doing business with our company.

In the digital marketplace, it's the *experience* our stories create which inspires consumers to become customers.

Business storytelling isn't a luxury for those with time and the inclination: it's the crux of differentiation.

7 Secrets of Storytelling Success

"Stories are the currency of human relationships." ~ Robert Mckee

It's our story that sells.

Storytelling is embedded in the human DNA. Before human beings were putting their stories on cave walls, they were passing along survival strategies through stories. We know this.

Fast forward to today, and consider how much we are willing to pay to experience a great story. Have you been to the movies lately? You're going to pay $12 (that's before a drink, some popcorn and a date), and sit in an uncomfortable seat surrounded by 100 strangers just for the opportunity to experience a great story.

We don't even blink at $10 for latest best seller for our Kindle. My wife and I recently paid $250 apiece see Justin Timberlake live in concert (It was worth it). A couple of live performance theatre tickets are going to set you back at least a Benjamin, and you'll still be sitting at a funny angle or really far away.

But then, have you ever seen *Les Miserables* on Broadway? Or read the entire series of *Game of Thrones*? Or seen *Avatar* in IMax?

We yearn for the Great Story. I'm a huge fan of science fiction (think *Ender's Game*) and high-fantasy novels (*Game of Thrones*). When reading a well-told story, there is an imperceptible moment when your mind unconsciously stops reading and instead begins to project a movie against the front of your skull. You're no longer sitting on an airplane or lying in bed. Time bends, and three hours later you look up, pissed to have been shaken from the story.

When it comes to a great story, cost, time and effort don't matter. We crave the emotional journey of a well-told story, and the opportunity to experience one is worth the price of entry every time.

I promise, I'm not trying to sell you on the notion that your content marketing efforts must mirror the best stories ever told. However, the most successful content marketers have figured out that tapping into the human desire to connect with a story is an extremely powerful method for business success.

The stories we tell shape the way consumers react to our brand. This is why content marketing works. This is HOW content marketing works. Our business storytelling creates the path which guides consumers directly to our doorstep.

Yet when it comes to corporate blogging we fail miserably at storytelling, with common leadership pushback including:

→ Stories are seen as unprofessional.

→ Stories can be misinterpreted.

→ Stories can offend.

→ Stories do not provide a direct ROI.

81

→ Stories rely too much on imagination and creativity.

And the most powerful pushback we receive from leadership:

→ Stories open the door to criticism and potentially-negative feedback, the digital nightmare of every corporate executive.

So we take every product or service we sell and create lists of functionality. We refer to our business in the 3rd person. We don't discuss individual staff members outside of their specific staff bio page. We never take a stance on any issue, nor do we discuss any topic in which we would could possibly have an actual opinion.

And, truth be told, at the beginning of my content marketing career, this was me.

After the success of the 100 Insurance Questions Answered campaign, I started creating a lot more written content.

We were getting a lot of attention from the 100 Questions Answered campaign, and with that attention came pressure.

"Never be scared of success, son."—Mike Hanley, my Dad.

For the first time in my life, I hit the brakes. I tried to produce content I thought was, 'a good representation of our business.'

It was terrible: bland and boring and direct and politically correct and watered down . . . it was impossible to provide any value. After so much success with the 100 Insurance Questions Campaign, once again I felt like an amateur content marketer, doing exactly what I told others not to do with their business blogs:

→ I used insurance 'insider' language and technical terms.

→ I used "The Murray Group" instead of "We" or "Us" or "I."

→ Every post was filled with information, but no personality.

Trying to sound 'Professional,' I was regurgitating insurance policy form information (and no one—not even an insurance agent—wants to read policy form information). Heaven forbid a client or prospect visit our website and be offended by a reference or opinion.

I got exactly what I wanted: I didn't offend anyone. I didn't piss anyone off. No one left negative feedback on our blog. No one started a Facebook page dedicated to hating on our business. Most importantly—

No one connected with us on social media networks. No one shared my articles. No one subscribed to our newsletter. No one picked up the phone and called us for an insurance quote.

I got exactly what I wanted: a professional, boring, non-offensive, useless online presence.

A month went by, then two months . . . then we were through the first quarter with ZERO success. I couldn't figure it out. I was writing three blog posts a week. I was sharing them on social media. We had an email newsletter that went out every month.

This content marketing stuff was supposed to work.

When we reached six months, I was about ready to give up. Why would so many intelligent marketers preach content marketing strategy if it didn't work?

Then I started to re-read old posts.

Awful.

I was ashamed. There is a clear and simple path to success using content marketing, and despite knowing, believing in and previously walking that path, I stepped off of it to go corporate. *Stupid.* I'm banging my head off the wall as I type this . . .

When I created each post, I thought I was creating something 'valuable'— yet I HATED reading them. I created these posts, and I hated them: they were mundane and ordinary and lacked energy (yes, insurance can have energy). And this is when I realized why I'd hadn't achieved any success:

No stories.

If insurance consumers wanted technical information, they could pull 83 their policy documents out from under the cabinet leg they'd been keeping level. If I was going help people become more informed insurance consumers, I needed to start telling some stories they could relate to.

I have no delusions that my stories could rival Tolkien or William Gibson. They didn't need to. I wasn't trying to capture a consumer's attention for hours, but rather just long enough to make an emotional connection. A few minutes, maybe even as short as a matter of seconds, was all I needed.

"Great stories succeed because they are able to capture the imagination of large or important audiences." ~ Seth Godin

A great quote from the powerful and mighty OZ—I mean Seth Godin. But one thing it's missing is the time element. In the business storytelling game, we don't need the same amount of time (at least not in one chunk) as a movie or concert or book.

Just a few minutes of captured attention at a time. That's it. If we focus on capturing the attention of our consumers, through story, just a few minutes at a time, over and over again, we can't lose. The heavens will open, the Sun will shine, and money will rain down from the skies.

Figuratively.

All we need is a moment of captured attention to win online.

So how do we tell a great business story? Here are seven secrets to business storytelling success I've seen work effectively. This is by no means an exhaustive list, but adding these particular seven "secrets" to your storytelling will drastically improve your content marketing results:

1. Be Subtle

Business storytelling must have a very subtle sell. Our story is meant build trust with the audience. Direct, overt sales tactics and solicitations DO NOT build trust. We use storytelling to attract new relationships, leads and sales over time. Business storytelling is a long-game play. We must be subtle in our desire for action.

The story must be spun in a way so that our Connected Generation audience feels they have chosen us, and not the other way around. The whole purpose behind business storytelling is lost when accompanied by an overt sales message.

Think about the political auto-response calls you receive every other year in November. A robot voice, calling from a blocked number, tries to explain why you should vote for a politician you may or not have ever heard of before.

This is hardcore, traditional interruption sales at its best (and worst). Do you appreciate receiving these calls? No, no one does. Even if you are excited about voting for the particular politician, there is nothing endearing about receiving a robo-call simply because you're a registered voter in that politician's district, county or state.

There is nothing subtle about a robo-call.

84

What if, instead of interrupting and disrupting the lives of her potential constituents, this politician instead works to tell the story of why voting is important? And, as part of that story, (told over the course of hundreds, if not thousands, of articles, interviews and speeches) offers voters of every political affiliate a simple service: A text or email reminder on election day to hit the polls for your favorite candidate?

Of course, this message would include the very subtle, "Courtesy of [Insert Candidate Name]."

Would you feel that your life had been interrupted or disrupted? No. You would have opted in to this service, and the message, though clearly sent from a candidate, wouldn't be pitching their platform, but rather thanking the voter for her or his participation in the one event (besides the Super Bowl) which clearly defines us Americans.

I don't have any hard evidence to back up this hypothetical, as I couldn't find any example of a politician creating a voter reminder service. However, it conveys the opportunity to potentially transform the general opinion of an industry, such as politics, from distrust to appreciation.   85

2. Be Specific

Our story must be specific to one segment of our audience. This is a transcendent content marketing principle. If we attempt to address every member of our audience with every story we tell, failure is the guaranteed result. Write one story for one segment of your audience. Then repeat this process over and over again, till every segment of your audience has been addressed.

If your storytelling is too broad, no one in your audience will connect with the message. The result will be a significantly diminished return.

Think back to the InsureMyFoodTruck.com case study. The actual business Denny Christner owns is BayRisk Insurance Brokers, Inc. He created the InsureMyFoodTruck.com brand as way to stand out by telling a very specific story to a very specific audience.

There is nothing about the name or brand of BayRisk Insurance Brokers, Inc. that speaks to a food truck owner. However, with effort and focus,

Denny was able to create a very specific brand that would resonate with the audience that he wanted to serve.

3. Be Authentic

Business storytelling doesn't work using "Corporate Voice." Your storytelling work must be done in the first person. It must be *your* voice, with your words and your cadence. Don't try and recreate a formulaic process that may have worked for someone else. **Your story only works if it's yours.** Authentic doesn't necessarily mean casual; its means honest to who you and your business are.

In the next section we take a deep dive into how you can harness authenticity to tell a more powerful story.

4. Be Honest

Don't inflate your success. This bears repeating, **DON'T INFLATE YOUR SUCCESS.** Writing a story about "going viral," claiming you received 100,000 visitors in a day when you only received 5,000, will eventually come back to bite you.

We all want to impress people; we all want to liked, to some degree. This is especially true when it comes to potential customers.

Maybe exaggerating business statistics or success doesn't resonate with you: you'd never dream of doing such a thing. Your moral compass points due North. It's possible—and more power to you. But I'm sure, at some point, you've been asked a fringe question by one of your customers or peers, and instead of simply stating, "I don't know," you try to piece together an answer from stats or experiences you vaguely remember.

Maybe you've name-dropped someone you don't know that well, or passed off another's story or idea as your own. Or maybe you inflate your own status inside your company, industry or organization.

These are natural human tendencies everyone fights when we want to be held in higher esteem by those we think matter.

When it comes to creating content, content that exists on the Internet *forever* (which you must assume all content does), you must be honest and accurate in what you publish. The one caveat is your opinion, in which case all you need to do is state that what you're publishing is your opinion and not to be taken as fact.

If you don't, and the audience catches wind of your dishonesty (and *do believe* that will happen eventually) all credibility will be lost, and no one will believe your stories again.

5. Be Brief

If your story can be told in 750 words, don't tell it in 1,000. Brevity is a powerful and appreciated weapon in your storytelling arsenal (admittedly a weakness of mine, just not in this section. Ha).

6. Be Relatable

You know your audience (or at least the audience you'd like to have). Your stories should mix in locations, activities and vernacular that your specific audience (or desired audience) can relate to. We want our readers to place themselves in our story, and believe they are part of it.

87

When I first started writing about insurance, as you would expect, the content was very dry. Rarely did I receive any social shares or comments beyond the occasional business associate who'd do me solid and comment, "Nice post."

These posts were tiresome to write and, I'm sure, even worse to read. As I started to feel more and more comfortable with the technical act of writing, I began to interject small pieces of who I am as a person into the content. My first ever personal reference was to being a Buffalo Bills fan. (For those not familiar, the Bills are a sports franchise in the National Football League, known most notably for losing four straight Super Bowls in the early '90s.)

I believe that it says something about a person if he can remain a fan of a sports team that suffers decades of losing, including losing four straight Super Bowls.

What's amazing is that people responded. They didn't comment on the insurance topic I addressed in the article, but rather some quip or story that related to the Bills or football or simply sports in general.

One simple reference took me from a stuffy, boring insurance guy to a relatable, everyday kind of guy my readers were comfortable engaging with.

7. Be Direct

Don't beat around the bush with your story's climax. We're using storytelling to sell our products and services to grow our business. If the resolution to the problem we described in our story is a product or service you sell, then you must tell the reader *and direct them to your solution*. Don't assume that readers will infer your product is the solution. You must direct them to the call-to-action, or they will not take it.

Mixing Number 1 ("Be Subtle") and Number 7 ("Be Direct") is an art form. You're going to have to do the work and figure out what the right mix of subtly and directness is for *your* audience. I'm sorry, I know that's a crappy answer, but it's the best I have.

In some pieces of content, you can be bold and upfront with what you want people to do; in others your call-to-action might only be a passing thought in the "P.S." section of your blog post.

→ The Rub

You don't need to have a PhD in 17th century British novelists to spin a story that sells your products and services online. Sometimes, it can be as simple as retelling a memory from childhood, or an experience you had helping a client the day before. Your stories don't have to be long, nor must they be filled with vast, unimaginable successes to sell your products.

The trick is to keep your eyes open in everyday life, and begin to see the stories taking place in your life that will help you to harness storytelling— and ultimately make more sales.

Authenticity

"Our business is infested with idiots who try to impress by using pretentious jargon." ~David Ogilvy

We hate the word "Authenticity."

What does it mean to be "Authentic?"

We tell ourselves we hate the word "Authentic" because it's been played out, used up and worn down by every business, every marketer and every salesperson who's ever given advice online. But, deep down inside, we hate the word "Authentic" because we don't believe we are authentic or, worse, we don't believe we are capable of ever being authentic.

We hate the word authentic because of our own insecurities.

I should know; I used to deal with this anxiety every time I hit publish.

"Is this article supporting my brand?"

"Is my take on this topic unique?"

"Oh, god, not another list post—is this really my best work?"

"Is this post too long?"

"Does anyone care?"

"Will this article help anyone *do* anything, or is just filler crap?"

The list goes on and on. Every article. Every time I hit publish.

Please, please, PLEASE someone hit the 'Tweet' button so I know you love me!

Sad. Pathetic. Lame.

Seth Godin, Marcus Sheridan, Mitch Joel, Gini Dietrich, Jay Baer, Joanna Penn—these thought-leaders are already killing it every single day, in every way imaginable. How can an upstart content marketer like myself standout?

Where do 'the rest of us' fit in?

How can we be different when the Internet is already filled with amazing, provocative, original thinkers?

It's true: there are many amazing minds producing content online today (and more every day). It can be hard to visualize your story standing out from all those who've come before you.

Don't try to be me. Don't try to be Seth Godin. Don't to try be Marcus Sheridan or Gini Dietrich. Don't try to be your favorite sports star or musician. Don't try to be your favorite author or movie star. Don't try to be your favorite teacher. Don't try to be your best friend.

You are about to learn the secret of these success stories, and that is: Authenticity is mandatory. Originality is NOT.

You are you. Be you.

90

The mixed-up, mashed-up, mess of awesomeness that makes you the most unoriginally authentic person in the entire world.

Be *that*, and you win.

Originality is often confused with authenticity.

Authenticity:
of undisputed origin; genuine.

Originality:
the ability to think independently and creatively.

Authenticity and originality are different animals.

If you want to grow an audience, to grow your business, if you want them to love you or at least respect you, **you MUST be authentic.** The thoughts, ideas, concepts, and beliefs you're sharing in your work must be true to who you are, the business you're trying to grow, and the goals you're trying to accomplish.

There is no requirement for originality.

"The privilege of a lifetime is to become who you truly are." ~ C.G. Jung
This isn't to say that originality doesn't help. It does. A lot.

When you can pull it off.

But all your audience really wants is *you*. Not some filtered, half-erased version you've conjured up because you think it's what you're supposed to be.

"Why, when we know that there's no such thing as perfect, do most of us spend an incredible amount of time and energy trying to be everything to everyone? Is it that we really admire—perfection? No—the truth is that we are actually drawn to people who are real and down-to-earth. We love authenticity, and we know that life is messy and imperfect." ~ Brene Brown

» Ego and Authenticity

One of my major failings in life is ego. I want to be famous (or at least wildly popular). I want to move people. I want to help people. I want people to want to hear what I have to say. Popularity was my motivation. At least it was.

At the beginning of my journey as a content marketer (the work you now see around my Content Warfare brand), I wanted so badly for people to notice me. Sitting here today, it kinda makes me sick to think about how badly being "Popular" online meant to me.

I followed who I perceived to be popular or famous online, and emulated their work. I learned everything I possibly could about what they did and how they did it.

Nothing happened.

No one visited my website. No one asked me for interviews. No one invited me to speak at events. I was a speck of dust in the Internet Universe, undeserving of mention.

I was writing in a voice that wasn't my own, and you could smell how inauthentic my work was . . . like garbage day. Its so easy to become blind when playing the Popularity Game. I was comfortable pushing the limits of content marketing when wearing my insurance hat. But when my marketer hat went on for my own business—when I played that Game—I began a lemming.

» The Cadence

(NOTICE: Here's how I solved my authenticity problem. As with every piece of advice in this book, it's the solution that worked for me. It may or may not work for you, but I encourage you to give it a try anyway.)

Fed up with what I was creating, I started to reread my articles, one by one. Whether out of boredom, idiocy or genius (which one, I do not know), for some reason I began reading them out loud.

It was immediately apparent what was wrong.

92 Inside us all is a natural cadence.

A rhythm.

A drumbeat that taps along as we create.

Mine is mine. Yours is yours. Everyone has their own unique cadence.

Authenticity happens when you find your rhythm, your drumbeat—your cadence. You could be saying the same shit that everyone else says, but if you *believe it*, if you say it the way you say things, *in your cadence . . .*
. . . that's all your audience wants. That, my friend, is authenticity.

Find your cadence. It helps to read your writing out loud. Does it sound like you? Do you hear yourself in the words the way you've written them?

No? Delete and start again.

Do this until your writing, read out loud, sounds just like you. What you're going to find is that, naturally, out of your cadence comes an ability to write and tell stories you didn't realize you had.

It will take time, no doubt. At first, you might still not feel authentic. But I promise, if you keep searching for your cadence, you will eventually find it, and when you do you'll forget about silly words like authenticity and originality.

For there will be no other way for you to tell your stories than the exact way that you do.

Dodging Bullets

I feel the need to apologize. You're a little more than half-way through this book and I haven't yet given you the formula to winning at Content Warfare. I'm sure, for some of you reading this book, a formula is the reason you decided to read it. You want see to the template for success, so you can thoughtlessly replicate and move on.

For those of you who did read this book for a formula, I now have to disappoint you.

I can't give you the formula to success.

I can't tell you what to say, write or create.

No one is going to hand you a script containing the exact words to attract your perfect audience, your perfect subscriber, your perfect customer.

You won't find the script in any $99 PDF download.

You're not going to find the script in a book or a newsletter or YouTube video.

There isn't a content marketing, copywriting or storytelling professional on the web that can hand you the script for success.

Truthfully, I hope a script isn't what you're searching for. I hope that your belief that a scrip is not the answer is what inspired you to purchase this book.

But if a script is what you're looking for, then unfortunately you're wasting a lot of time.

Stop searching for the script.

Scripts, formulas, and fool-proof strategies are dead (if they ever lived). They don't work. Not today. Maybe yesterday; but today, no. Not because there is anything intrinsically wrong with scripts, formulas and fool-proof strategies. Rather, the speed at which content mechanization techniques proliferate on the web make it impossible stand out. The Internet culture is too eager to curate and share successful ideas.

This is the reason good business storytelling wins at Content Warfare. Tactics get played out faster every day.

You have to stand out.

Long-form, short-form, fan gate, whiteboard explainer video, eBooks, visual reinforcement . . . none of it matters if the audience your content is intended for never actually sees it or, even worse, sees it and doesn't care.

Scripts are bad. Formulas are bad. Focusing on tactics is bad— unless your script, formula and/or tactics are backed up by a great story.

But tactics, scripts and formulas—fool-proof strategies that are not backed up by a great story—will always lose in the end. Eventually, your audience will realize you're using these gimmicks, and all the trust you've built will be destroyed.

Think about your own experiences.

Once you know something is part of a systemized scheme, you start to feel a little dirty—and most likely hit the 'back' button. There are two caveats which will allow you to look past the yucky feeling you get from this type of content:

1. Demand.

If your product is in enough demand, you can write your content on the wall in monkey poo, take a picture of it, then post it on your blog, and sales will still come in.

2. Trust.

If people love you, hanging on your every recommendation and product offering, then no matter how you display it, sales will come in.

Here's the deal: you don't need to develop the next talking Elmo doll, or spend 15 years building up unshakable customer loyalty in order to generate new leads from your content marketing.
Just do you. Be authentic.

If you have to use some script, tactic or formula, don't be sneaky about it. Be transparent.

You will stand out because of who you are and how your work makes people feel . . .
. . . not because of some long-form sales page script or systematized email campaign.

Embrace creativity.

Tell your story.

Educate your clients.

Help without expectation of reciprocation.

Be consistent.

This is how you stand out. These are the basic concepts on which you build your platform, creating inevitable differences between you, me and everyone else creating content to communicate, build relationships and ultimately influence the buying decisions of Connected Generation consumers.

Stop searching for scripts and formulas! Just do 'you,' over and over again.

A better way to read your favorite blogs.

Like many, I'm a huge James Altucher fan. The guy is just smart. Smarter than me, for sure. Plus, he's been worn raw through years of failures and successes.

If I tried to mimic his mix of intelligence and self-deprecating humor, I'd sound like a jackass.

James Altucher stands out because he's true to today's version of himself, and he's wildly popular for it.

Brent Kelly, the independent insurance agent who founded Empowering Sales, is NOT as popular as James Altucher with the masses (not yet, at least), but he's held in the same esteem to those who regularly read his work.

But if you try to emulate James, or Brent, or me, or any other one of your favorite blogs, you'll certainly fail.

One person's success is NOT gospel for the world.

Here is a better way to learn from your favorite blog:
Read everything, take what works for you, use it, and throw everything else in the garbage.

Take your favorite blog down off the pedestal, and cherry pick the ideas that work for you.

That's the secret. Cherry picking. Create some new concoction of awesomeness distilled from the best bits from your favorite 37 bloggers, photographers, journalists, video creators, talking heads, musicians, artists, CEOs, toll booth operators . . .

. . . whoever. You're building the best version of yourself, just like playing with Legos.

97

That's why scripts don't work.

Someone else's words, someone else's process, someone else's formulas CANNOT be the best version of you.

My advice: be frivolous at first. Cherry pick from everyone and anyone who lights you up. "Steal like an Artist," as Austin Kleon would say.

Over time, take notice of what feels right, of what your audience responds to, and make the necessary adjustments.

Your content is a homebrew of exactly what you put in it.

→ Now: start adding ingredients.

#

Another reason we search for formulas and scripts to help us tell our story is out of fear. **Fear of "the block."**

Have you ever sat down to write, and your fingers wouldn't move?

The ideas are there, waiting in your brain.

Your notes are ready. You've got a great headline.

Your office is even quiet for once.

The setting couldn't be any more perfect for you to craft a meaningful, thoughtful, valuable piece of content your audience will enjoy.

Except nothing happens.

Nothing.

This isn't how it's supposed to work.

The words are just supposed to come to us. You have the knowledge inside your mind; why isn't your internal librarian pulling the proper sources?

Where are the words?

Why aren't my fingers moving?

Then things really start to spiral:

What if I don't have my blog post ready for tomorrow?

What if I don't get a new post out this week?

What if I never write another blog post again?

AAAHHHHHHH!!!! Why won't my fingers work?

» **Ruthless Writer's Block**

Despite having written more than two thousand blog posts in my career to this point, I experienced (about six months before this book will ultimately be published) one of the most ruthless episodes of writer's block I've ever dealt with. At least when it came to writing new blog posts.

I had a few strong excuses:

> » I was deep in the pre-order campaign for the Content Warfare Book.

> » I was in the process of transitioning out of The Murray Group to start my own content marketing consultancy.

> » For some insane reason, I decided to add a second weekly episode to the Content Warfare Podcast (I called these 'Content Warfare Unplugged').

Not to mention I had a six-month-old in the house, which drastically decreases productivity.

99

These are excuses. And as legitimate as they may be, they have nothing to do with writer's block.

We all have excuses for not getting our writing done. When excuses start to stack on top of excuses, the pressure to publish mounts, adding to the anxiety of NOT hitting publish.

You know that moment: when someone asks you a point-blank question, something you know, something you know very well. . .

. . . and the answer is just gone?

It's as if writer's block has a gun, and it's pointed right at your head.

We freeze. We hesitate. We second-guess ourselves as if our life truly is on the line.

Take a deep breath.

Not posting to your blog is NOT the end of the world, the end of your business, or even a reason to have a bad day.

Writer's Block is NOT Creativity Block

Over the course of finding your audience, telling your story and winning the battle for attention online, you're going to create a lot of content.

There is nothing we can do about writer's block. It's going to happen. Whether you're writing the next *Game of Thrones* series or a blog post for an insurance agency, there are going to be times when the words just don't come easy.

In these moments you have two options:

Option #1: Keep Writing

Joanna Penn, bestselling thriller novelist and a former guest on the Content Warfare Podcast, shared that she doesn't have a problem writing, and she doesn't worry about writer's block.

Why?

Because she's trained herself to plow right through it. She doesn't view writing as a task she hopefully can find some time for; writing is an everyday activity she prioritizes alongside breathing air. Granted, Joanna is a writer, so this makes sense, but if you plan on capturing the full value of content marketing, then writing every day is a best practice.

Even if the writing is terrible and off topic, write. You're developing muscle memory.

Option #2 : Stop Writing

Reevaluate what you consider 'content.' For many companies, a blog post is 500-750 words of text, and an image. That's it. That's what they consider content, and there is nothing wrong with that.

During my weeks of not being able to post new text-based material on my blog (because of "the block"), I didn't stop creating: I simply changed the medium with which I told my story. Instead of text-based content, my audience received two YouTube videos on content marketing, and six new Content Warfare Podcast episodes.

"Writer's block" isn't "creativity block." Find new methods to spread your message.

So your fingers won't work?

Start talking into a microphone.

Don't have a podcast?

Publish your audio tracks to Soundcloud. It's free, and easy to embed inside a blog post.

→ The Rub

The reality is that your audience doesn't care if you deliver your value via a text-based blog post, a podcast, a video or an image. They just want valuable content that is going to help them.

101

You dodge the writer's block bullet by getting out of the way.

Don't just sit at your desk and stew about the words that aren't coming out of your fingers.

Move.

Action is the only answer.

You can't dodge the writer's block bullet by standing still.

→ **Now get to work.**

7 Simple Tips to Create More

Let's say you choose Option #1: Keep Writing when experiencing "the block." It's not going to be easy. But there are methods for creating more, valuable content.

Derek Halpern, online entrepreneur and founder of Social Triggers, would tell you (and I agree) that most bloggers and business owners create way too much content. However, I don't feel it has anything to do with the frequency of posts.

Frequency of publishing is NOT a variable in the equation of content *value*.

Most bloggers and business owners create way too much self-indulgent, self-oriented content.

Remember the 3 Cs of business storytelling? Only one of the circles has anything to do with you or your business.

Here is where the problem lies: We create content valuable *to us and our business*—and then wonder why we're not getting traction.

This type of content, regardless of technical quality or professional production, has almost NO value to the clients and customers for whom the content was intended. Self-indulgent, self-oriented content wastes your time and that of every blog visitor who is unfortunate enough to come across it.

So what does valuable content look like?

Valuable content provides simple answers to everyday questions.

Content marketing isn't rocket science or marine biology. Content marketing is the process of answering the questions our current and potential customers have about the product or service we provide. If I've said it once, I've said it a thousand times:

Content marketing works—it's just work!

The 100 Questions Answers campaign taught me that.

Let's be clear on something, I'm not advocating you produce a new piece of content every single day. Unless you're competing against TMZ or the New York Times, posting with such frequency is not necessary.

Every time I tell the 100 Questions Answered story, I get questions about how I've been able to maintain quality and volume at the same time. The answer lies in the lessons learned from my work producing that campaign. I did so many things wrong during that project.

What you find below are the lessons I learned. If producing larger volumes of content is important to your business and telling your story, the following 7 tips will help you find success.

7 Simple Tips for Creating Valuable Content Every Day

1. *Create an Editorial Calendar*
The worst possible scenario? You show up each day and don't know what you're going to write about. Confusion distracts you from the work of content production. No matter how many days in a row you plan on posting fresh content, have a topic or idea scheduled ahead of time.

103

2. *Video is Your Friend*
How long does it take to get a two minute video posted on YouTube? Answer: about 20 minutes (from recording to editing to uploading). How long does it take you to write 500 to 750 words? Longer than 20 minutes for sure. Video is easy. Video will humanize your brand. And Google loves video, especially YouTube.

3. *Stay on Topic*
Group similar sub-topics of information together as best you can. This was a big mistake I made with the 100 Questions Answered campaign. The topics of questions I answered were random. This made it hard to remember what I'd said previously and how I said it. This also created a disjointed feel to the project as each video was published.

4. *Steal Like an Artist*

In his book, *Steal Like an Artist*, Austin Kleon gives us permission to pull thoughts, ideas, and strategies from peers, competitors and even sources outside our own industry for use in our own work. He's not talking about plagiarism or copyright violations, but rather the assimilation of successful concepts. We can do this and maintain our authenticity. Your unique voice and brand is a mixture of everything you surround yourself with. Trust me, at some point you're going to need inspiration.

5. *Work in Batches*
This was the biggest mistake I made. I tried to produce a new video each day. HUGE MISTAKE. Take a day and record 10 videos (or write 2-3 articles, record 7 podcast episodes, etc.), then package them all up for publishing. You will thank yourself for this preparation. Too many things will pop up each day providing excuses for NOT getting content out. Batch creation is exactly what John Lee Dumas does for his daily Entrepreneur on Fire podcast.

6. *Use a Formula*
Trying to recreate the wheel with each post is a sure path to burnout. Have a formula to your posts. A nice simple formula might look like: Headline, Image, Intro, Video/Podcast if using these forms of media, Transcription, Call-to-Action, Recap, Done. Don't worry about each post looking similar. The video is what you want them to watch anyway, and most people scan posts. Many will actually appreciate the consistency.

7. *Have a Purpose*
This is a big one. Don't create content simply to create it. That's silly and a HUGE waste of time. Only take on a project of this nature if there's a specific goal you wish to achieve. For the 100 Questions Answered campaign, mine was inbound new lead phone calls. Make sure visitors to your content know what you want them to do.

Here are two bonus tips for those of you using video:

> » Embrace Your Flaws – Don't get messed up about "ums" and "ahs." Try to limit filler words like these as best you can, but remember, much of power behind answering questions is displaying your ownership of the knowledge. A little human error is fine (and, in some cases, appreciated).

» Solicit Help — If you take on a project with this level of content production, you're going to get burned out. I did. Have days where someone else gets in front of the camera. In general, this is good for branding, and it will help you regain some sanity.

I want to stress: I don't believe you NEED to create fresh content every day. But if you do so, while maintaining a high level of value to your customers, the results will blow your mind.

Become the Competition

"When you focus on innovation, you become the competition."
~Daniel Burrus

I don't follow tech trends very closely. This may sound crazy, but I don't geek out on the latest technology stuff. I grew up in the woods of Upstate New York, creating fictional worlds in the forest behind my house. Technology had little impact in the games we played.

That doesn't mean I don't love the Internet.

I do.

I love the ease of communication and the accessibility technology affords us, but as far as gadgets go, such as the next wave of smartphone—

I couldn't care less.

106   I'm a storyteller.

I'm a content marketer.

I believe that if you focus on delivering value with every piece of content, the result will be stronger relationships than you could have ever imagined and, ultimately, an endless stream of opportunity (foreseen and unforeseen).

If technology helps me do this, I'm all for it.

But we don't need technology to tell great stories.

So I don't read Daniel Burrus's newsletter for the technology stuff. What I admire about Daniel Burrus, why I think his newsletter is such a fantastic resource, is because he is singularly focused on innovation.

I love innovation.

I try to read, listen to, watch and meet innovators as often as I can. I try to infect myself with the innovators' spirit, energy and ideas.

In a 2013 newsletter, Daniel Burrus writes on Google and their social media efforts with Google+:

"This is where it looks like some mistakes started to occur, because Google shifted their focus from 'innovation' to 'beating the competition.'"

"One of the problems of focusing on the competition is that you end up competing with them. In contrast, when you focus on innovation, you become the competition. That's a big difference."

Let's take Google, Google+ and social media out of the discussion. The point isn't whether or not Google has made mistakes in its creation and integration of Google+. It doesn't matter what was, or what was supposed to be. What matters is what is—and what Google+ is today is an incredibly robust and engaged network of social connections.

<u>Becoming the Competition</u>

There is an important lesson to our content marketing work that can be pulled from this quote:

107

". . . when you focus on innovation, you become the competition."

That's a very powerful thought.

We see this every day. In the insurance industry, some would have said that my competition includes GEICO, State Farm, Progressive, Nationwide, All State, and other mega-companies that spend ridiculous amounts of money to advertise their insurance products (GEICO spent over $1 billion in 2013).

Do you think it's possible for a small independent insurance agency in Upstate NY to "beat" any of the companies just named?

Shit, no. It would be impossible.

Well. . .

It would be impossible if they were actually the competition. There is no chance for small business to beat the mega-companies, no chance at all, if we play their game.

If we try to beat the big boys in the advertising game, we lose every time.

So, if we have no chance to beat our Big Box competitors, what are we as small business professionals and entrepreneurs supposed to do?

We friggin' innovate

We become the competition.

We small business professionals . . .

We entrepreneurs . . .

We solo-preneurs . . .

We main-street, real-life, community-based businesses . . .

WE BECOME THE COMPETITION!

108 . . . and it all starts with our story.

Content marketing is the innovation.

To me, figuring out new, effective, exciting, engaging, emotion-driving, revenue-generating ways of telling the small business story is *innovation*.

Because our story is the Ace in the Hole. Our Big Box competitors don't have a special story. They don't have a community to rally.

Innovation is figuring out how to deliver your story in a way that integrates into people's lives, instead of interrupting those lives.

This is Content Warfare.

When you use content marketing to innovate your story and how you tell your story, you become the competition.

No one else has the story you have.

No one else can tell your story the way you can.

→ **Get your hands out of your pockets, and get them on the damn keyboard.**

WIN
THE BATTLE FOR
ATTENTION

"It takes courage to give away something of value without expectation of immediate return" ~ Jay Baer

I'm often asked, in interviews and speaking events, about where the Content Warfare brand came from. The asker of this question is often hoping for a grand and amazing story, such as: "I was fired from my job and I had a spiritual awakening and a this genius idea hit me and . . ."

Unfortunately, the real story is kind of disappointing. It wasn't a moment or event; there wasn't a chance meeting, or sage advice from which Content Warfare was born.

Content Warfare is the standard for those who gauge their success over the breadth of their lifetime work.

What we do as content marketers, storytellers, business owners, entertainers, podcasters . . . what we do for a living, every day, with every piece of content, is to battle for the the attention of those who would grow our business.

The name Content Warfare just seemed the natural derivative of this belief: creating a body of work, one piece of content at a time, that cannot be ignored.

We grind, day in and day out, battling, winning each new audience member one at a time. Victory, success, achievement—these never happen overnight. There is no trick to success.

There is you, and there are the obstacles that stand in your way. We each wage a war inside ourselves every single day, to do the things that need to get done, to hone our craft, to make connections, to prepare ourselves for some moment in the future, some defining moment that will only lead to more defining moments till one day we will lift up our heads, look around, and feel satisfaction—

112   Only to put our heads back down and get back to work.

We work to create content that can't be ignored. Content that demands attention. And it is that attention, the currency of the Internet, that allows us to create the life we care to live.

Out of this was Content Warfare born, and to the victors go the business-growing attention we've battled so hard to win.

What is Attention?

What does attention mean to you?

Attention – to regard someone or something as interesting or important.

Attention – the cognitive process of selectively concentrating on one aspect of the environment while ignoring other things. Attention has also been referred to as the allocation of processing resources.

How do we convince our audience to "selectively concentrate" on *us* "while ignoring other things?"

We don't convince them. We *inspire* them. We entertain them. We educate them. We provide so much value in the content we create that the idea of your audience giving attention to the competition is silly.

Size of audience, amount of attention . . . numbers don't measure success. For some, success comes from attracting the attention of ten True Fan customers, while for others that number might be ten million.

Remember our discussion on audience. What's important is not the size of our audience, or the amount of attention we receive: you win the battle for attention online when the right audience gives you nothing more than the minimum amount of attention necessary to become a True Fan.

Attention

Attention is the currency of the Internet.

Not views, not "Likes," not subscribers, but attention.

Online business thrives on attention; it's our sunlight, our electricity, our rocket fuel. If we cannot attract and retain attention to our brand, our business stagnates, withers and, if left unchecked, perishes into the cyber oblivion.

On the surface, those who have attention come by it easily. Take a megastar like Beyonce. She walks the street to a chorus of shutter snaps as every fan-boy and -girl waits with bated breath for a look in their direction.

Even celebrities within the marketing niche (like Seth Godin) attract attention with ease. If Seth picks up a pen to sign a credit card slip after lunch, we marketers lose our minds in the hope he'll scribble some transcendent marketing idiom upon the receipt.

From the surface, attention comes easy to those who have it.

But it didn't always, and won't forever.

We must work for attention and, once we have it, must work to keep it.

Entertainers like Beyonce and thought-leaders like Seth Godin are true Content Warriors. And both understand the reality of content marketing success.

Though they may not phrase their efforts in this manner, each has been fighting the battle for attention their entire career.

Believe it or not, there was a time when the world didn't know Beyonce or Seth Godin. Neither was picked or chosen, or born into some special club.

As author James Altucher would say, each has flourished in the "Choose

Yourself Era" by clawing and scratching and fighting for every drop of attention they could get.

Each is talented, no doubt. But neither's talent alone attracted the attention they respectively enjoy today.

They're workers.

This is what Beyonce and Seth Godin understand, that many who struggle with attention do not.

Attention, the currency of the Internet, the keystone of content marketing success, is held by those who last.

» Flash-in-the-Pan Attention

Talent can attract attention. Raw talent, especially, can attract attention. (Everyone is interested in the new, shiny object.)

Consider the NFL Draft.

So much attention is given to rookies—players who have not played one NFL snap, yet we throw them a party.

Thousands of NFL fans from all over the country travel to Radio City Music Hall in NYC to watch their favorite team draft seven players.

There are 52 players on an NFL roster. The vast majority of them go unheralded, but statistically will contribute more value to the team than the attention-grabbing first-draft picks.

We love raw talent. We're willing to give our attention away for the opportunity to witness greatness take its first step.

But this type of attention is fleeting. It's flash-in-the-pan. In a breath, attention given is taken away.

Yet some will base their entire content marketing strategy on attracting "bursts" of attention. This is a strategy I would advise against (at least for those marketers and businesses who have yet to establish their base of True Fans).

Attempts at viral videos, one-off infographics and small-budget paid ad campaigns are all examples of flash-in-the-pan attention grabs that always end up wasting more resources than they produce.

The battle for attention online is won with each new drop in the bucket. Seth Godin has done this by blogging every single day for seven years: meaningful, sincere, forthright ideas and thoughts shared every day—for free.

Or consider Beyonce's husband Jay-Z. At 17, he was selling crack cocaine on the streets of New York. At 44, he's one of the most successful entertainment brands the world has known.

In his book, *Decoded*, Shawn Carter (more commonly known as Jay-Z) explains his relentless drive to push his message and brand forward. Album after album, new sound after new sound, Jay-Z wouldn't allow his audience to forget him by constantly exploring what it meant to be a hip-hop artist.

116 An incredible talent for sure, but there are many incredible talents in the music industry. Jay-Z commands attention unlike any other in this industry because his goal was to outlast his competition.

Jay-Z has many projects that, on their own, would stand as a successful music career. But taken together as a whole, the attention Jay-Z receives as an artist compounds over time.

Each new project builds upon the success of those that have come before. The result is more capacity for failure and testing.

It may seem like attention comes easy to some. But **attention is an asset, cultivated over a career of failure and testing and growing and learning and doing it all over again.**

Attention given quickly is attention quickly taken away.

The converse is also true (Yes, we can say and do something so egregious that our audience is no longer willing to give their attention to us for philosophical or moral reasons). But the longer we hold our audience's attention, the easier it is for our audience to give more of it.

They're sold. They're invested. You and your message, your values, become part of who they are.

Declaring yourself a Content Warrior means more than just writing, shooting video or recording podcasts.

You're tethering yourself to the grind, to the art, to the pursuit of creating meaningful work which attracts lasting attention.

Content Warriors are not to be trifled with, for they have put in the time, built the network, and earned the value equity that keeps their audience coming back to experience each new project.

Seth Godin has written over eighteen books.

Jay-Z has recorded thirteen #1 albums.

→ What are you going to do?

Where Attention Used to Be

"For someone with a print background, you're accustomed to the fact that if it . . . gets into the paper, you're going to find an audience," she said. "It's entirely the other way around as a digital journalist. The realization that [the audience is] not going to just come and read it has been transformative." ~ Janine Gibson, editor-in-chief of the website The Guardian.

When I was a kid, Sunday morning was all about the newspaper. By the time I got up, my Dad was below the fold: three sections deep in our local newspaper.

Sports, Business, Politics—the section didn't really matter. I don't think he was so neurotic that he read the paper in a consistent pattern each week. But as I'd bounce out of bed, there'd be my Dad, cup of coffee steaming on the kitchen table, newspaper in hand.

After we exchanged "Good Mornings," I'd sit down to eat my breakfast and my Dad would begin to regale me with his opinion on the stories he had read prior to my waking.

At age ten, much of what he said I didn't really understand, at least not the gravity of how the issues impacted our lives. But what I did become acutely aware of was that stories reported in the newspaper were important.

More than that, the newspaper was important for telling the stories that needed to be told.

With the decline of traditional print media throughout the U.S. over the last decade, it's quite obvious much of my generation (Gen Y— I'm 33 at this book's publishing) and those even younger do not feel the same way about newspapers the generations before us did.

Newspapers require active reading and attention. Maybe, we've just grown complacent.

In a recent study done by the Newspaper Association of America, print-only newspaper revenue in 2013 was the lowest it's been since 1950 (approximately $20 billion) and is continuing to fall. Digital revenue only adds another $5 billion to the total. A far cry from the $65.8 billion in total revenue the newspaper industry enjoyed in the year 2000.

For centuries, the newspaper industry has held an authoritative positive in consumer minds in terms of where to find quality providers of products and services. And for good reason: for most consumers, there was no other method to stay informed. Options were limited.

I'm not about to discount the quality of journalism that takes place within the newspaper industry. I hold journalists in very high esteem. But it's undeniable that the "News Now" world we live in has begun to look at options outside the newspaper industry for content to consume.

What many traditional newspaper publications have forgotten is that the "newspaper" part of their business is just a medium for delivery. The point most traditional newspapers missed is that they were never in the newspaper business to begin with: They were in the *attention* business.   119

Yet, somewhere along the line, they lost sight of this goal. Instead, they put the idea of the physical object (the newspaper) ahead of what their business really does: report and comment on the news.

What's the moral of this story? **Forget about medium and focus on message, or you'll forever be slave to medium.**

Not to say that medium isn't important. But medium of communication is only important after you have a story to tell; when you know who your audience is and the message you want to share with them.

This is why, more than halfway through this book, we haven't yet discussed any particular medium for telling your story. The tactics and strategies associated with any medium often cloud our ability to distill an incredible story worth sharing with our audience.

Twenties years ago, America got its news from the daily paper and evening

TV news. Today it's YouTube and Yahoo. Tomorrow it will be something different.

The platform or medium our audience utilized to consume our content is of little relevance. If you know who your audience is and the story that must be told to attract them, negotiating the inevitable platform will almost seem natural.

Long-Form vs Short-Form

This is the way I see attention evolving:

You can go deep on content. Dive into the research, do the interviews, find the solutions, ask the questions and provide uncompromising value.

Or . . .

You can go shallow and deliver bite-sized pieces of immediacy. Be the headline business, the ticker-tape business.

Neither is wrong. Neither is the solution.

But you have to be one or the other (or be smart enough, nimble enough and scaled enough to do both).

The in-between doesn't work.

No one cares about short-form content that isn't immediate, or the half-assed long-form content that doesn't solve problems.

We all must choose.

The Work is Never Sexy

"Don't bunt. Aim out of the ball park. Aim for the company of immortals." ~ David Ogilvy

Do the work. Leave the excuses!

On January 2nd of 2012, I started answering insurance questions, using my cellphone video camera, one at a time, every single day, for 100 days. I posted those answers on YouTube and then my insurance agency's blog.

I had no idea what I was doing. The lighting was awful, the sound was terrible and the backdrop was ugly. I didn't know how to edit the videos, nor did I have any idea how to format a "video show."

I did everything wrong.

Except for the fact that I did it.

Content marketing works. But it IS work.

The work of creating 100 insurance videos in 100 days was not sexy.

By the 30th episode, I was worn out. By the 60th I hated the project. On day 70 I started telling myself it was a waste of time. By day 80, I believed it. By the 90th episode I almost quit. I told myself no one cared. I told myself no one would notice the work and that no one would call even if they did.

In the drudgery of cranking out a new video every single day, the incremental increases, the small wins didn't materialize in my mind.

I couldn't see the forest through the trees, as the saying goes.

When I reached episode 100, it was time to take stock of what minuscule achievements we'd accrued.

Except, as a body of work, the results weren't minuscule at all.
YouTube views increased by over 1000 percent. Our website traffic went up by 300 percent, and we had booked more than $5,000 in revenue directly

attributed to the YouTube videos in a little over three months.

On its own, no single video even slightly moved the needle.

But taken as a body of work, I had just changed the course of my business forever.

If you can understand this one concept—that **effort is one of the key variables to success in content marketing**—you will drastically increase the overall value of your business and brand online.

Small wins add up over time.

It takes time for your audience to find you.

It takes time for Google to find you.

It takes even more time for your audience to trust you, and more time after that for Google to trust you.

Page views are sexy. New email subscribers are sexy. New sales are sexy as hell. But the actual work of content marketing that acts as the catalyst to page views, email subscribers and sales is not sexy.

There is a saying I like to use when discussing content marketing in front of an audience: "The juice is worth the squeeze."

Grinding out catchy headlines and article ideas day after day is hard work, but the business-growing attention you receive from consistently pumping out more value than your competition will blow your mind.

The Art of Professional Content Marketing

I'm often asked about content marketing shortcuts. "How do I get to where A-lister so-and-so is—in three months?"

Write more content. More crap-free content, that is.

There is a core issue preventing content creators within small and mid-sized businesses from producing the content that grows their business.

They see themselves as amateurs. This is the obstacle to content marketing success we're here to overcome. This is the obstacle keeping you from attracting the attention your business needs to grow online.

Content Warfare is a book about winning your own personal battle, the internal struggle you face every day to create high-quality content.

If you want to win the battle for attention online, it's time to stop thinking of yourself as an amateur.

I can say this because I was an amateur once, too. I can tell you the exact day that I stopping being an amateur and went pro: January 2, 2012.

123

On that day I allowed myself no more excuses for not making time, or focusing on non-content generating activities. On Jan. 2, 2012, I began the *100 Insurance Questions Answered in 100 Days* video campaign and became a professional content marketer.

Many small and mid-sized businesses don't even have official marketing departments. The marketing function is often just a bullet point on a job description, not a respected organizational pillar driving growth.

No matter where marketing falls within your organization, regardless if you're creating content full-time or at 11 p.m. after the kids go to sleep . . .

Today you turn pro.

We've now reached the point where we transition from "why" to "how." Take this journey with me.

Believe that content marketing is vital to the future success of your business and seize this opportunity.

As Jeff Goins explained to me in an interview we did for the Content Warfare Podcast, "Life will never slow down and provide the optimum scenario to become the pro version of ourselves."

We must decide to do so—and then take action.

In an effort to win the battle for attention online, we, as content marketers, must take to our keyboards, video cameras and microphones with reckless abandon.

Plan. Produce. Proliferate.

I'm not talking about cluttering the Internet with crap content.

This is a common misconception held by many content marketers. More content is NOT the answer to attracting more attention. WRONG!

This is our amateur brain trying to finish a task instead of working to accomplish a goal.

Content marketing is NOT about *more* content, it's about more content that is useful, entertaining and/or inspiring to your target consumer base (starting with your True Fans). Valuable content doesn't involve the word "Epic" or "Awesome" or any other trivial adjective that describes nothing. Valuable content doesn't have to go viral.

Valuable content educates, entertains or inspires (preferably all three), and does so in the language of the consumer.

Simply capturing one of the facets of valuable content can lead to success. This is exactly what Denny Christner did at InsureMyFoodTruck. com by using Twitter to connect and educate food truck owners about their insurance needs. Denny educated his consumer. This is why the 100 Insurance Questions Answered campaign worked. I used the language of the consumer to educate them on their insurance needs.

Now think about the success of thought-leaders Seth Godin and Gary Vaynerchuk, not in terms of their audience size, but in the voracious nature of their fan base (myself included on both accounts). The power that Seth and Gary wield oozes from their ability to create a message that at once educates, entertains, and inspires their audience to take positive action in life and in business.

The first step in transitioning from amateur to professional in content marketing is dedicating yourself to never again shove your sales pitch down the throat of every poor sap willing to connect with you on social media.

When you educate, entertain and/or inspire your audience, purchasing your product simply becomes the next logical step.

This doesn't mean you don't have to sell. You do have to sell. If no one purchases your product or service, then you won't have a business for very long.

What professional content marketers know (that amateurs do not) is that the sale must be subtle in order to capture the Connected Generation consumer.

The average consumer sees 1,500 to 2,000 brand impressions a day. If your [125] content marketing message starts with "Buy now" how do you expect to stand out?

Why should they buy?

Better question, "Why would they buy?"

It's only going to be a matter of moments before this same consumer sees a brand message from one of your competitors, saying the exact same thing.

Your value proposition is NOT your latest sale or discount.

This is why Denny Christner took to Twitter and began conversations with food truck owners, why Seth Godin has authored over 18 books, and why Gary Vaynerchuk spit wine into a Jets helmet for over five years.

Most likely none of these men, (especially Denny Christner, who's an insurance agent by trade), would self-identify as a professional content marketer. But all of them are, because of their effort to educate, entertain and inspire their audiences with every piece of content they create.

I know you believe in content marketing. That's why you're reading this book.

→ It's time to become a professional.

7 Basic Principles of SEO

We understand now that the professional content marketer isn't going to shove her latest sale down the throat of the audience she's trying to serve. So let's begin to take a more tactical look at content marketing—specifically, the role that SEO (search engine optimization) plays in content marketing success. I'm not an SEO expert by trade, nor do I pretend to be one, but in the world of content marketing a basic understanding of core SEO principles is paramount to success.

The basic principles of content marketing are almost too obvious. We've referenced all three already in various ways throughout this book:

1. Use keywords, literally and deliberately.

2. Deliver more value than your audience expects.

3. Deliver value often and consistently.

Yes, this is an incredibly watered down version of content marketing. But if you had no other information on which to build your content marketing strategy, these principles (in time) would take you to the promised land.

The basic principles of SEO are slightly more technical. For that reason, I'm going to do my best to use high-level concepts and terms we can all benefit from, regardless of our current level of understanding.

The Penguin and Panda Google updates have created a digital world, where optimizing your content for people trumps the old-school SEO methodology of optimizing for bots, that once dominated the digital marketing industry.

That being said, here's a few timeless principles of technical SEO that will have an immediate impact on your ability to get content found in Google Search.

Target mid-tail and long-tail keywords first.

Long-tail keywords are longer and more specific keyword phrases (usually three or more words) that visitors are more likely to use as they near the point of purchase.

Targeting mid-tail and long-tail keywords will not yield higher traffic volumes on a per post basis but will, instead, return the more qualified traffic.

It may seem counterintuitive, but this strategy is particularly powerful for content marketers that need "Early wins." Long-tail keywords have significantly less competition, as the vast majority of marketers create content around traffic volume alone.

However, the sexiest part about long-tail keywords is their influence on conversion rate. According to a study done by Conductor Research, website pages with long-tail keyword optimization have a conversion rate 2.5 times higher than standard keywords.

Remember the Content Warfare process: find your audience, then tell your story. It's hard to share content valuable to your target audience based on generic keywords. Using long-tail keywords allows you to target the specific topics most valuable to your target audience.

If you are just testing content marketing as a strategy for your business and you have to report results to a boss, targeting mid-tail and long-tail keywords would be a strong recommendation.

Your boss doesn't have to know you only got 50 hits on your blog if five of them turned into sales.

Use keyword synonyms throughout your articles and website.

Regardless of what future Penguin, Panda or other search engine updates have been pushed through the system, SEO best practices will always be focused on providing the humans visiting websites with a better experience upon their arrival.

This being said, stay away from repeating the same keyword phrase over and over again. This is practice commonly known as "Keyword stuffing."

The Penguin and Panda updates to Google diminished (if not completely removed) the necessity to stuff your website with a single keyword in order to rank.

Webmasters used to fill strange places on your website, (i.e., hidden headers, footers, body text areas) with repeated keywords to improve the volume of keyword usage while minimizing the impact on the user experience. Don't do this. You can now actually be penalized for such activity.

Google is looking for natural keyword density, written with the purpose of delivering value. No one in the natural course of writing or speaking would use the phrase "New York Workers Compensation Insurance" 15 times in a 450 word article.

Today, with the increased relevance of semantic search, Google is now smart enough to understand the usage of keyword variations. Always, always, *always* err on the side of providing a better human experience, versus trying to 'game' the system. In this case, the juice is NOT worth squeeze.

129

Per our example above, use variations like "NY Workers Comp," "Workers Compensation in New York," or "Workers Comp Insurance" where those variations make sense.

Build upon your successful articles and pages.

Using a tool like Google Analytics, it's possible to track which articles are performing the best on your website. If you find that a certain blog post or page on your website is performing extremely well, consider going back and adding onto the article.

What does 'performing well' mean?

This could mean many things, or just one—it all depends on the goals of your content. Performance metrics could include new email subscribers, leads, event attendees (webinar or in-person events) or even sales (though, as we've discussed, sales are long-game in today's marketplace).

Using simple goal conversions in Google Analytics, we can track which pages are turning website visitors into each specific success metric.

Once we've identified posts or pages which are experiencing success, it's prudent to build upon that success. In these cases, either your audience or Google is telling you that something you've created has value.

The worst thing you can do in this situation is let that success lie.

In 2011, I wrote an 1,700-plus word article titled, "If you work in insurance, this is the only article you'll ever need read about the future of social media." The article was immediately a hit with my target audience (insurance agents). Within my first week of posting this article, it became the most-read blog post I'd ever written. I had over a dozen syndication requests, hundreds of social media shares and 50 plus comments.

Now, I could of just chalked it up to good timing and writing and moved on to the next thing. But is getting off the launch pad enough? Why not send the ship into orbit?

130

When we have a hit article, don't sit on it. Build on it. Take the subject deeper, chop it up and repurpose everywhere you can, make the article even more valuable than it already is. Here are just a few ways to build on a hit article:

1. Take as many individual ideas from the post as you can and expand upon them in additional articles. Spread these "Breakout" posts between your own site and other relevant sites who are willing to accept a guest post. Always link back to the original article as the genesis of this new piece.

This creates more links and traffic pointing at your original article.

2. Repurpose the article into other forms of rich media. This could mean doing a video or video series on the topics within the article, a podcast episode, a slidedeck posted on Slideshare. Repurposing your content in this way makes the concepts available to an entirely new audience that prefers to consume their content in different methods besides the written word. Again, we're always linking back to the original article.

This creates more links and traffic pointing at your original article.

3. Dive back into the article and expand/update the information. I've done this twice now with the article referenced above. Once to add some additional stats and evidence and once to expand and update some of the ideas I shared in that article. Things change over time (especially in the marketing industry) and for your article to continue being a relevant, valuable resource to both Google and your audience it's important to keep the article contemporary.

As a result of going in and updating my post, in both instances it's been reinvigorated, reaching new eyeballs, attracting new social shares, and more importantly, contributing to the success of my business (via new email subscribers).

It's important to note that updating, editing and expanding on high-quality, deep resources that aren't performing well is even more important. This won't often be the case when you've spent serious time and effort on an article, but it will happen on occasion.

4. Do not try to rank more than one article for the same exact keyword.

131

A common mistake I see among struggling content marketers is keyword over-optimization. Keyword over-optimization happens when we attempt to rank more than one article or page for the same exact keyword phrase.

Here's how this happens with insurance agencies across the country: One of the primary products that insurance agents sell is homeowners insurance. Intuitively, it may make sense, that because you'd like to rank your insurance agency high in Google for the term "homeowners insurance," every article is about homeowners insurance. The term is stuffed into every article, sometimes every paragraph of every article.

Now, replace "homeowners insurance" with any product every sold online and replace "insurance agency" with any business that ever attempted to sell a product online. Because keywords used to play such a large role in SEO success, keyword over-optimization is a pervasive problem, especially among small and mid-sized business trying to DIY their content marketing.

So, what's the problem with keyword over-optimization? We cannibalize our keyword ranking. If every page on your site is optimized for the same term, how does Google know which article to serve in search? Which is the most valuable and deserves traffic? This practice is confusing to your audience and Google.

This is why long-tail keywords was the first principle on this list. Long-tail keywords allow us to attack deeper topics within the same general topic without sacrificing our traffic for any specific keyword phrase.

Here is a keyword categorization system that has worked for me over the last few years:

>> Primary Keywords - These are core keywords of your site. These are the trigger words for consumers looking to buy your product. Set up pages and/or landing pages dedicated to each keyword or keyword phrase specifically.

>> Supporting Keywords - These are often long-tail keyword phrases that add onto your core primary keywords. Most of these keywords will be addressed through blog posts.

>> Orbiting Keywords - These are keywords that aren't directly related to your core business and aren't associated directly with your primary keywords as to be supporting. Often these are keywords outside your specific industry that attract the same kind of consumer. An example would be an insurance agency writing articles about mortgages. An insurance agency doesn't sell mortgages, but consumers interested in mortgages also need insurance.

5. Internal linking tells Google that your old content is still relevant.

Internal linking may not deliver the same "Google Juice" as external linking. However, using a consistent internal link strategy is important for sending Google bots (and your human audience) deep into your website to older posts which still contain value. A good internal linking strategy also helps describe keywords that should be applied to internal pages through the words used in the link.

Think of supporting and orbiting keywords as the leafs of tree facing out into the world, collecting attention and traffic for your brand. Internal links are the branch system distributing that attention and traffic throughout the ecosystem of your tree and root system. Each new supporting and orbiting article provides new opportunity to send your audience deeper into your site.

This can be incredibly valuable when you've identified the pages most successful at converting attention and traffic into leads. Use internal linking to reinforce both the technical and human SEO of that page by sending more and more traffic there.

There are two pitfalls to avoid when it comes to internal links:

» First, like keyword usage, don't over link. Keep the links natural where they make sense in the context of your content. It may seem obvious to state, but planning opportunities to link to your higher converting pages is solid and winning strategy.

» Secondly, avoid linking to different articles for the same phrase. As we've discussed this type of activity will confuse both your audience and Google. Confusing either is bad for your overall content marketing success.

6. Build a natural mixture of external links into your highest converting content.

Link building is NOT dead. Depending on when you're reading this book, mentioning this may or may not be necessary. But as of the writing of this book, Google updates Penguin and Panda have caused some digital marketing guru-rockstar-ninjas to proclaim link building dead.

Maybe not. Gaming the system with low-quality paid links is dead. Creating a portfolio of high-quality, relevant links from established and respected websites is still very powerful and very much an important aspect of search engine optimization.

There are many different types of external links including strong, relevant keywords from sites ranked well for a similar keyword or keyword phrase all the way down to cheap, shallow link farms with a thousand links on one page. Though I would encourage you to stay away from the very bottom of the external link spectrum (as that gets into a no-longer fuzzy black-hat SEO region that can cause serious harm to your website's performance) it is very important to diversify your external links.

I would, however, recommend a strong emphasis towards links from targeted sites with a long history and deep, quality content. These are obviously harder to get as everyone targets websites of high quality, (a good example in the marketing industry would be Copyblogger), but they do hold a lot of weight.

You know your industry and the websites with respect and power within that industry. This could be trade publications, digital magazines, traditional newspapers digital publication, peer organizations, government or non-profit organizations. Links from these types of websites, who often achieve their status by discriminating in the quality of content they publish, provides Google with a valuable indicator of your website's quality. However, these websites often take quite a bit of work and relationship building to get featured on or a guest post opportunity from.

Because quantity of links is also important (not the be-all-end-all by any means, but important), I recommend targeting sites with a lower barrier of entry as well. This could be local chambers of commerce, small business partners or bloggers inside your industry.

These smaller organizations, often whose largest struggle is finding quality content, will most likely to be more receptive and quicker to respond to your content contribution inquiry.

Link building is a huge topic. There are entire books dedicated to the topic. For purposes of this book, **focus on a high-quality, diverse link portfolio and NEVER pay for links.**

7. Use words for their literal meaning

For as sophisticated a system as Google has created, Google bots still don't get sarcasm (this may change over time as semantic search grows in influence). Now, I enjoy a cheeky headline as much as the next guy. But if you're writing content for the purpose of getting found in searches, you need to use deliberate, literal language. The language of the consumer.

This manifests itself in a couple different ways:

>> **The first is headlines that don't let your audience grasp what the article is about.** These are usually short, sarcastic, or humorous headlines which don't actually describe what the article is about. The common rebuttal to this in the marketing industry is Seth Godin. Seth Godin's blog post titles are often non-descript and/or mid-thought. Here's the deal: Seth Godin is Seth Godin, a New York *Times* best-selling author of over 18 books who've been blogging for over a decade.

There is a chance that your audience will respond to these type of headlines (most likely not, but it's possible). Unfortunately, you'll never get found in search.

>> **The second is using industry language that consumers don't know or understand.** This includes acronyms. Don't use acronyms unless the acronym is widely known and commonly used among your audience. A common example of this in the insurance industry is the term "Full coverage." Anyone who's everyone bought car insurance has used this term. When I used to sell insurance I can't tell you how many times I heard someone ask for "full coverage." Except "full coverage" doesn't actually exist. There is no such insurance coverage. Yet consumers use this term every day to describe the amount of insurance coverage they have.

135

The mistake that I see so many insurance agencies make is that they don't address "full coverage" in their content marketing. These agencies explain comprehensive coverage, collision coverage and "Other Than Collision" coverage, the official coverage names of what consumers call "full coverage."

Think back to the story about my worn calipers. I had a "right turn squealing" problem. My buddy the mechanic's website listed that his auto body shop fixed worn calipers. If he wasn't my buddy, he would never have gotten my business, because he wasn't using the language of the consumer.

He wasn't using a cheeky headline, but he wasn't using the language of the customer. I had no clue what a worn caliper was before he told me. There was zero chance of me putting the term "worn caliper" into Google in finding a provider for my car issue.

This also doesn't mean you can't use funny headlines to entertain your audience. By all means: be funny. Just understand that those aren't the headlines that are going to help you get found in search (though legitimately, those types of headlines may help you with social sharing). You have to choose what the goal of your post is, then create a headline to help you achieve that goal.

→ The Rub

Done right, following these basic principles of SEO, your business will have a much better shot of getting found in search at the exact moment consumers need your product.

Remember how this chapter started.

Deliver value first, always. Before all other things, create content that is valuable to your target audience. Master that skill while following these basic SEO principles and you'll build a solid foundation to generate more inbound leads.

Love the Grind

*"It hurts doesn't it? Your hopes dashed, your dreams down the toilet.
And your fate is sitting right beside you." ~ Teddy KGB, Rounders*

Have you ever been good at something and given up the moment it stops coming easily? For most of my youth, I was a pretty good baseball player. I always made travel teams, started every game and when the time came, I graduated from high school and moved on to play college baseball for the University of Rochester. I talked baseball every day. All my friends were baseball players. Baseball was more than just something I did, it was part of who I was. But when I got to college, the story changed a little.

I learned quickly my freshman year that pitchers threw harder, could break off curveballs for strikes and change-ups that fooled. The competition was elevated quite significantly from high school. For the first time in my baseball career, I struggled.

Something that I loved so deeply suddenly became a job. I stopped enjoying the game. Practices were no longer fun. I didn't go for extra batting practice and I didn't take extra fly balls in the outfield. I blamed baseball for my struggles, instead of myself.

137

"Baseball is ninety percent mental and the other half is physical."
~ Yogi Berra

Content marketing, much like baseball, is for grinders.

Baseball is a grinders game. Those who succeed in baseball are not necessarily the most talented. To succeed at baseball you need to love the grind. Every day on a baseball field is not going to be easy. The very best in the sport, the most celebrated hitters of our national pastime, fail seven out of ten times at bat. It takes a certain kind of individual to press on through a 70 percent failure rate.

And for a brief period in my life, my entire freshman year of college baseball, I forgot what the grind was like. I forgot about the small wins. On a baseball field, success is measured by a series of small wins. This is why everyone is so superstitious. If you've struck out two at-bats in a row, simply making contact and fouling a ball off in your third at-bat is a success. Small success piled on top of small success leads big success. It could take two weeks to get out of deep slump in baseball. The only way back is grinding through the failures one after another.

By the grace of the Baseball Gods, I was surrounded by an amazing group of guys. Many of which became my friends for life. They put me back to work doing the activities and drills a baseball player does. They reminded me of the grind it takes to succeed on the baseball field. Ultimately, my sophomore, junior and senior years were successful.

Creating great content is no different.

In order to be successful in content marketing, you need to love the grind. Not every blog post, video, podcast, image, message, call-to-action, landing page or marketing campaign that you create is going to be successful. In all honesty, you will probably fail more than you succeed, especially at the beginning.

On the baseball field we talk about celebrating small successes. Often times you can go two or three games in a row without getting a hit. During these times, it's hard to feel like you're part of the team or that your work is meaningful. But when you do get that first hit after a slump, that small success has to be celebrated. Success in a grinder's game, like baseball and content marketing, is about embracing and holding onto the positive. Know that your worth is ultimately not determined by any one action that you take but rather the body of work you produce over your career.

Five Methods for Learning to Love the Content Marketing Grind

1. Set milestones between where you are today and your ultimate goal. There is nothing that makes you want to give up on a goal more than looking at a task that seems insurmountable. When you write a month's worth of blog posts and check your Google Analytics account only to find an insignificant gain in visitors, you're going to want to quit.

Lesson: By setting incremental goals between your start and where you want to be, the small increases in counting numbers will seem like success. As you hit each new incremental level, you'll be reinvigorated to reach the next one.

2. Block out time in your schedule every week for content creation. When you're not seeing the success you expect, it's easy to begin to make excuses as to why you do not have time to create content. Non-revenue generating tasks creep into your daily routine (content marketing should be considered revenue-generating) as a distraction from putting in the work.

Lesson: Block out times in your schedule for content creation which ensures you will continue to write,even on the days that you don't feel like it.

3. Don't write in a linear fashion. When we embark upon the journey of content marketing, our goal is to find our audience, tell our story and win the battle for attention online (which will ultimately lead to revenue). But attempting to tell our story in a linear fashion from start to finish can create roadblocks. The creative side of our brain was not built to travel in a straight line.

139

Lesson: Use practices such as mind mapping and outlining to sketch out your story. Then work on the sections that come to you the easiest first. With the overall structure mapped out, you don't have to worry about missing crucial sections.

4. Ask for feedback. Our mind can be a dangerous place when left to its own devices. Creating content in a vacuum, without the feedback of others, can create a false sense of failure. We begin to ask ourselves dangerous questions: is anyone reading this? Am I worthy of telling this story? Are my words having any effect on people? Does anyone enjoy my writing? All these questions bring doubt into your content creation.

Lesson: Ask for feedback from your audience at every stage of the game. What is connecting and what isn't? I promise you, at least one person out there loves what you create and will enjoy telling you so.

5.   Read the content you create out loud. Any content worth creating is going to have some sort of voice. A simple trick that I use is to read my work out loud to myself. If I like the way the content flows and moves when it's spoken, then I know that someone who's reading it is going to enjoy it as well. Find your cadence and rhythm. A much deeper connection will be made with your audience.

Lesson: There is something special about hearing the things you've written come alive in the spoken word. There is a rhythm and personality different from being read in silence

Bonus » Surround yourself with people who love to create content. As I explained from my own experience with baseball, the only thing that brought me back to the game was surrounding myself by other guys that loved baseball and understood what I was going through. I've also found this in my content marketing work.

Lesson: Find a mentor or join a mastermind group, online or in-person. You are going to need a support system. People who don't create content will never understand what you're going through.

→ Don't Let the Grind Get You Down

I promise, even if you take all six of the methods I listed above to heart and embrace them fully, at some point in your content creation journey you're going to want quit. The grind is going to wear on you, you'll fall into a slump and something that felt easy and enjoyable will become work. In these moments, you choose whether to become a professional content marketer or stay amateur. The professional understands that slumps happen and finds ways to love the grind regardless. The amateur gives in to the temptation that things should be easy, believing that success is impossible.

Knowing When to Downshift

"Comedians tend to find a comfort zone and stay there and do lamer versions of themselves for the rest of their career." ~ Chris Rock

We all want to get our digital marketing into fifth gear as fast as possible. Fifth gear is overdrive, where we can hit cruise control and glide along at top speed and optimum performance. In terms of content marketing, fifth gear is amazing. Our content marketing strategy attracts high-margin prospects, our social media outposts build deep, sustained relationships and our email marketing automation drips value, turning prospects into repeat customers at an industry leading conversation rate.

Here's the catch with fifth gear (anyone who's driven a manual transmission vehicle will understand this completely):

Though fifth gear may be the highest speed, it's also the gear with the least torque. Torque is the rotational force at any given point around an axis. In layman's terms, torque is the force of your tires pushing against the ground, moving your vehicle forward. A 2013 Porsche 911 Carrera can go from zero to sixty miles per hour in 4.2 seconds. In comparison, a Toyota Prius goes from zero to sixty miles per hour in 10.1 seconds. The Porsche has a lot of torque. The Prius does not.

141

» Shifting into Fifth Gear Too Fast

You can't simply shift from first to fifth gear. Shifting into fifth gear too early is a common mistake/misunderstanding of companies struggling with content marketing. They want to be in fifth gear before even starting their marketing engine. This is impossible. Regardless if you are in a Porsche or Prius, you have to make your way through each gear, one by one, before reaching cruise control. Attempting to skip a gear results in failure every single time.

The reason you can't skip gears?

Not enough torque. First gear has the most torque. First gear takes your business from no movement at all to forward progress. First gear creates momentum. Second gear has slightly less torque than first, but a higher speed building off the initial momentum created by first gear. This process continues until you reach cruising speed, fifth gear, the lowest torque, but the highest top speed.

If you attempt to skip a gear, your car will begin to buck and jerk violently. Without the proper momentum built up through the lower gears, the car will actually begin to lose speed despite being in a higher gear (remember, higher gears have less torque. Without proper momentum, they are useless).

» How to Build Torque in Your Content Marketing

I am in no way suggesting that you need to spend a lifetime in each gear of your content marketing campaign. But it is going to take time. It took Brian Clark and his company Copyblogger Media years to get the traction they enjoy today. Here's when you might be doing some downshifting in your content-marketing vehicle.

First Gear: Strategy and Branding Objectives

If you don't know where you want to go, how do you expect to get there? Many companies just beginning to take their offline business into the online world skip this step. They're doomed to failure before their key ever turns the content-marketing ignition.

Every action you take from this point on should be dictated by the strategy and branding objectives set forth. When marketing my insurance agency, I had a little sheet of paper next to my desk with five objectives on it. If a marketing action didn't meet one of those five objectives, I didn't do it. It was that simple. If I came across coolest idea in the history of marketing, but it didn't meet one of our strategy and branding objectives, it didn't happen.

Thinking of first gear as the filter every piece of content you create must pass through before going into production mode. You can have as many strategy and branding objectives as your business needs and your content creation bandwidth allows.

One of my primary branding objectives at the insurance agency was to establish our business as a thought-leader in our local market around the topic of "Business Leadership." We wanted to create discussions short-term and a digital community long-term of local business leaders discussing all things leadership.

We chose this as a branding objective, because one of the insurance agency's main product lines was commercial insurance. By attracting the attention of local business leaders, we were essentially creating a seat at their table. We wouldn't have to push our way into conversations anymore. Instead, we'd be leading the conversations on platforms we either controlled (our blog, social media) or that we had access to (Facebook groups, Google+ communities). As an example, one of our most successful blog posts in terms of branding, engagement and social sharing was titled: 17 Leadership Characteristics the Boss Expects You to Know.

This passed through our filter on multiple levels. Employees who wanted to be leaders were interested to find out what they may not know. Current leaders (the "boss" as we called them) were intrigued by what they should expect their employees to know.

When creating strategy and branding objectives for your content, don't think in terms of what you want (more sales), **think in terms of who you want to interact with** (business leaders, in our case).

Second Gear: Content Foundation

Your content foundation will serve as the basis of everything you do moving forward. The posts are often referred to as "Pillar Posts," deep resources showing your expertise on a topic.

This early-stage content sets the tone and direction of what your digital marketing presence will be. Every post you create in the future will build upon your foundation of pillar content.

For this reason, the creation of strategy and branding objectives is so vital and reinforces the necessity to not skip gears. If you don't build a content foundation, you find your message scattered and content creation meandering and ineffective.

Suppose your business was retail shoes. One of your pillar posts may be focused on Women's Running Shoes, "The Ultimate Guide to Purchasing the Perfect Women's Running Shoes." You spend serious time on this article, whatever it takes to explain every facet of the Women's running shoe buying process. Put your expertise on display so it is clear to anyone reading your article that you are a solution-provider worth considering. Pillar content should have a more broad focus than standard blog post. The intention is to deep-dive an entire category of content. One of the primary purposes of pillar content is to rank the article for broader, higher-value keywords.

Each subsequent and supporting article on the topic of Women's running shoes attacks the long-tail keywords associated with the topic. These articles might have titles such as, "How to choose the most comfortable winter running shoe," "The 10 best all-purpose women's running shoes," and so on. Allow your one pillar post to work on broad keywords while your supporting blog posts find pockets of consumers doing more specific searches. Make sure to always link to the pillar post somewhere in the supporting blog articles, so that both humans and search engines know that your pillar post is the most valuable resource on your site for women's running shoes.

Then, repeat this process for each major product, service, course, content category on your site.

Third Gear: List Building

Once you've defined your strategy and branding objectives and begun executing on those objectives starting with pillar content, it's time to begin capturing the contact information of individuals who are drawn to your message. In the online world, this is most commonly done through email.

There is no better way to get a group of individuals to take a given action in a given period of time than email marketing. Without a quality email list of people who believe in you as a value creator, future projects will struggle to gain the momentum they need to be successful. Want to publish a book? The individuals willing to give you their email address are going to be the first to purchase. Want to start consulting? Your email list contains all the pre-qualified leads, the people who have given you permission to send them messages.

If you see an article with the headline similar to "Email Marketing is Dead," believe that person is either link-baiting or an idiot.

Email isn't the only form of permission-based list building. There is also SMS (Text message). Google+ has list building built in, yet today (and for a far into the future as my crystal ball can see) the true value in list building remains in email.

Fourth Gear: Community Building

Online communities come in many different forms. There are membership sites, where the community is built inside a website. The most obvious and straight-forward communities are on social media networks, LinkedIn Groups, Facebook Groups and Google Plus Communities. Then, there are the communities that are not encumbered by a medium, but rather an idea or interest. These types of communities tend to orbit around different hashtags. The most popular being #starwarstuesday and #caturday. Like them or hate them, these are incredibly powerful communities with a ravenous appetite for more content.

Communities empower your audience to engage and allow each individual voice to be heard on a more intimate level. As the owner and/ or moderator of a community, you move from expert to authority in the eyes of your audience. You no longer are just pushing your content out to a group of interested individuals, you're feeding the discussion and moving it forward by highlighting the work of other successful thought-leaders in your industry. Take your email list further and build a community of like-minded people around your expertise.

Fifth Gear: Conversion

Fifth gear is where you start selling your products and services and also where so many businesses fail. Most of us do a little strategizing, create some content, maybe even do some list building but then try to skip all the way to conversion. Yes, there will a few sales made this way. But if you're interested in sustainable results and repeat clients, you must give each gear its due time to generate momentum. There is so much information available online about how to convert traffic into sales. If you take the time and work your way through each gear, building upon the momentum of the previous gear, you won't need to chase conversion tactics. Sure, there are some basic conversion best practices, but tactics don't mean squat if you don't have an audience that trusts you.

The audience you build, taking each gear through its due course, will be clamoring to buy your products and services. You'll have proven yourself as a value creator. Then, one day without realizing it, you'll be in cruise control.

When to Downshift

146 On a straight road, in a drag race, this is the process of leveraging torque, building momentum and achieving content marketing success. But, the road to content marketing success is never straight. Likewise, the road to success in anything is never straight.

As marketers we're always striving for cruise control, that perfectly automated online process where we effortlessly deliver marketing campaigns that always yield a high return on investment.

I would be doing you a disservice if I pretended that this straight path to content marketing success was even possible. It's not. We have to prepare for the downshift. Some pillar posts aren't going to work, some communities don't materialize. Setbacks will happen. Instead of letting this derail our momentum, my recommendation is to downshift.

One common form of content marketing fail is over-expansion of social media network usage and tactics. Over-expansion is a curve in the road to success we're all going to face at one time or another.

It's so easy to chase the latest social media network to try and find new traffic. We have to be on Pinterest, right? And Twitter? And Vine? And

Instagram? And LinkedIn? And Facebook? And Foursquare? And Quora? And Google Plus? (Yes, you should be using Google Plus.)

Professional content marketers understand that we can't be a success on every social network. Michael Stelzner, founder of the mega social media marketing brand Social Media Examiner, once admitted in a podcast episode that he doesn't spend much time on Pinterest or LinkedIn. This is one of the most successful social media marketing blogs in the world today and founder isn't well-versed in two of the big five social media networks.

This isn't a failing of Social Media Examiner, but a focus on the tools which generate the most value for the business. We gain torque in content marketing through focus.

Pick one, three max, social network(s) that you will use to market your business and build authority on. That's it. If you decide that Pinterest isn't going to be one of those social networks, don't waste time there!

For me, I doubled down on Google+ about 18 months ago and it has catapulted my career. Twitter and LinkedIn round out my three social networks (I'm on Facebook but it's an afterthought.) But realizing that attempting to be an authority on Twitter, LinkedIn and Google+ is impossible, I choose where I did the best work, Google+ and planted my flag. Based on your strategy and branding objections, consider doing the same (not necessarily Google+, but pick three network with one primary to build your brand around). It's okay to have a presence on more social media networks, but make it known where you do your best work.

Additional curves may include:

>> Reduction in marketing budget, forcing you to pursue more bootstrap strategies

>> Technology failures forcing reinvestment in hardware and software

>> Changes in the search landscape, forcing adjustments in content marketing strategy

>> Loss of key personnel, forcing a change in the online voice of your

147

business

» Economic upturn or downturn forcing adjustments in overall marketing strategy

» Addition or reduction of competition, forcing new strategic alliances and partnerships

These are just a few of the speed bumps you may experience. The digital marketing landscape is constantly changing. We must be able and willing to take a step back and refocus, in order build up the momentum necessary to reach cruise control.

→ The Rub

There are two primary takeaways from this chapter: take your time and prepare for failure. Everyone attempts at some point to skip gears in our content marketing campaigns. It's very easy to do. We begin to feel a little momentum, things are going well and we want more, faster.

148

What separates a professional content marketer from the amateur is recognizing when their content marketing campaigns begins to sputter and jerk. At this point, amateurs just continue, attempting to push through and wondering why they never achieve the success they desire. The professional content marketer downshifts and refocuses till enough momentum is built to move on.

→ Don't be in a rush to get to cruise control.

Digital Sharecropping

"You must have a home base!"

You've heard this a thousand times from every blogging guru and social media ninja slinging advice throughout the digital world, myself included. The concept of creating content on digital properties you own, most often your website, is a cornerstone principle within the content marketing universe. When you own the digital property, no one can change the rules on you and negatively impact your business.

We've seen this with Facebook. Brands who have built their entire digital presence on a Facebook brand page are now scrambling to gain traction as Facebook's algorithm (commonly known as EdgeRank) continues to show less organic brand content in the streams of would-be customers (unless these businesses are willing to pay).

There was most certainly a time when a Facebook brand page could have been your most active and profitable digital property. Except you don't own Facebook. When Mark Zuckerberg decided it was time to monetize Facebook, business and brand pages went from community building tool to advertising platform. The companies that have been unwilling pay are getting crushed and will continue to get crushed.

149

This is the new normal for Facebook. There is nothing you, content marketer, can do about it. Facebook is a public company now. They have investors to answer to and must make revenue (increasing revenue) to keep those investors happy.

The issue is, so do you.

» If it Happened Once it Can Happen Again

It would be naive to think that this couldn't happen again on Twitter, LinkedIn, Google+ or even YouTube. Even small changes like YouTube moving to Google+ integrated comments had a dramatic impact on some YouTube creators' business.

When LinkedIn first opened up their publishing platform, I posted an article on my site banging on how the platform was being marketed to the general user base. The initial set of "LinkedIn Influencers" (a group of approximately 150 individuals including Richard Branson and President Barrack Obama) were attracting hundreds of thousands of views on every new published article. The LinkedIn Publishing Platform during its release to the general user base was being heralded as unprecedented opportunity to reach LinkedIn's built-in audience of business professionals.

My argument against the LinkedIn Publishing platform was twofold: One, you don't own the distribution (despite ultimately owning rights to the content). Two, the initial results of the "Influencer Program" were unsustainable once ability to publish long-form content was expanded from a couple hundred users to over a hundred million users.

My concern and motivation for writing the article was in the false expectations of unrealistic reach in an ecosystem where the rules could change at any time. I was worried small businesses in particular would give up creating on their own website in exchange for LinkedIn. This isn't to say that you should not be using the LinkedIn Publisher Platform (and Facebook, for that matter). Just that we need to create on these platforms with our eyes wide open.

» The Case For Digital Sharecropping

Digital Sharecropping is a term popularized by the content marketing site, Copyblogger, and provides a negative moniker to the practice of creating original content on digital properties we don't own.

From the first moment I heard of this concept, I believed it to be an absolute truth. Especially for mid- to small sized companies whose brands don't transcend the consumer public, like say a Coca-Cola or Red Bull. Creating any meaningful audience online is tough work. To do so, and then have our ability to reach that audience taken away by an algorithm change on a social media network can feel like a sucker punch to gut.

However, the ever-evolving digital consumer in 2014 has made me question the "absoluteness" of the Digital Sharecropping principle and here's why:

In a world of mobile humans, attempting to control where conversations happen is futile. Consider facilitating the conversation across medium and platform.

What's more important to your business, that potential customers visits your website or that the same potential customers develops a positive brand impression?

Tom Webster, VP of Strategy for Edison Research, appeared on the Content Warfare Podcast and explained the need for successful content marketers to create "multiple on-ramps."

Seriously. Think about it. Because common content marketing best practices would state that everything drives visitors back to your website. But what happens when potential customers don't want to visit your website? Think about your own mobile Internet use. Do you relish the idea of being taken out of the app you are using to someone's website? In most cases the user experience you get inside mobile Facebook app or LinkedIn or Google+ is exponentially better than whatever website you're going to be sent to.

151

In 2013, Facebook had over 189 million "mobile-only" users. Even if the website these users land on is mobile enabled or mobile responsive the content-consuming experience is broken up. This is that moment between clicking a mobile link and when the piece of content is ready to be consumed on the mobile device. This is a barrier. With every negative mobile user experience, our audience becomes less willing to make that leap out of social media platforms to our website (regardless if they are mobile or not).

This is what dogged me about Digital Sharecropping. Why would we deny our audience the ability to consume our message where, when and how they preferred? There is no doubt that your website should be your number one digital priority. You own it, you control it. No one change the rules on your website. But that doesn't mean that every piece of content your create must live there and there only.

We dedicated an entire section of this book to finding who you audience is and where they are. Is that effort for naught if you're not providing at least a somewhat-deeper experience for that audience on the platform they prefer?

» Where More YouTube Views Happen

This isn't just theoretical, marketing blather I've concocted to fill pages in a book. This concept has played out over and over on YouTube, specifically. From testing my own YouTube videos, I've found that driving people to YouTube to watch one of my videos produces significantly more views (in the tune of 10 times more views per video) than driving those same people to my website where a YouTube video is embedded. YouTube as a platform reaches more adults aged 18 to 34 than any cable network.

Your audience is attracted to YouTube for its ability to combine educational, entertaining and inspirational content with an easy to use format and integrated social function. Bringing our mobile discussion back, over 40 percent of YouTube global views come from mobile devices. Do you think the mobile video viewing experience is better inside YouTube's mobile app or on your website?

This being the case, why would we drive our audience to our website versus YouTube? The answer is, it depends on your goal. YouTube, though great for branding, awareness and audience building, traditionally has very poor click-through rates.

For the majority of my videos, (most notably my Google+ Starter Kit series), the goal is not visitors to my website, it's video views. I want my audience to watch, engage with and share the YouTube video. If I know from testing that this happens more when I send people directly to YouTube, then do I care where the views happen, as long as they happen? I believe the answer to this question is no. My goal is content consumption, not website hits.

There are lots of good things that can happen on my website that will not happen on YouTube, (new email subscribers, speaking inquiries, book purchases). The point is, **there is value using platforms other than your own website to provide content-consumption opportunities for your audience.**

Mark Traphagen, Director of Online Marketing for Stone Temple Consulting and Content Warfare Podcast guest calls this, "Tapping into Other People's Audience."

Jay Baer, founder and CEO of Convince and Convert, (also a Content Warfare Podcast guest) shared a similar thought in his recent presentation at a Social Fresh Conference titled: Shotguns Trump Rifles: Why Social Success is Now a Volume Play.

The premise of Jay's presentation was the value in social media marketing is "reliable reach," the ability for marketers to send a message to their audience and have that message actually reach their audience.

Jay explains that email, the telephone, even direct mail is reliable reach, but social media is not. Jay has over 124,000 Twitter followers. According to his Twitter analytics, if he sends out a Tweet, approximately 2,000 (or 1.6 percent) of those followers will see that Tweet. The issue stems from which followers see that Tweet. There is no way to target which 2,000 of Jay's 124,000 Twitter followers that Tweet will reach.

153

The solution, reflecting the name of Jay's presentation, is a shotgun approach to attracting attention. This creates a situation where Digital Sharecropping isn't a good idea or even a best practice, but rather a necessity for connecting your story with the audience it serves.

» Content Views and LinkedIn Publishing

Anecdotally, I've found the same principles of content consumption we discussed in regards to Youtube and the LinkedIn Publishing Platform. Although I have yet to run a formalized test similar to YouTube (where I found a 10-time return of YouTube platform views), it's fairly obvious from my LinkedIn article view counts that LinkedIn users enjoy consuming content from within LinkedIn. My first three LinkedIn Publisher Articles all received view counts in the thousands within the first week of publishing, where I may receive only a few thousand click-throughs to my website from LinkedIn in an entire month.

As with YouTube, if your goal is website traffic, then sharing into LinkedIn is the best practice. But if your goal is getting an idea in front of the maximum number of LinkedIn users, then consider creating from within the LinkedIn Publishing Platform.

→ The Rub

There is no doubt that both personal and business brands need to have a home base (website they own and control). Creating all your content on platforms you don't own is a recipe for disaster. Just ask all the small businesses that built digital presence solely on Facebook how they feel about that decision today. Digital Sharecropping without a home base is most certainly bad business and recipe for complete disaster.

However, once you've established that home base, reaching out and creating inside platforms such as YouTube, LinkedIn Publishing and Google+, can attract attention, drastically expand reach and rapidly grow your audience.

Original Content on Google+

In the last chapter we, dispelled the myth of Digital Sharecropping and explained why creating inside platforms you don't own (once you've established your home base), has become a necessity for attracting attention online.

Consistently creating original content inside of Google+ is a cornerstone practice to building an engaged audience. However, it is possible I'm biased, as much of my content marketing success is a result of the work I'd done of Google+. There is a reason I've spent so much time building an engaged audience within Google+. Google+ is a boss's social network.

Specifically, Google+ is the social media network of leadership.

Leadership — "a process of social influence in which one person can enlist the aid and support of others in the accomplishment of a common task" ~ via Wikipedia

...of thought-leadership

...of cultural leadership

...of economic leadership.

Google+ is a community of leaders, helping each other grow their respective reach and expertise in the topics they pursue.

» How to Google+ like a Boss

Soon, I'm going to share seven tricks that will get more people commenting, resharing and plus one-ing your original Google+ content. This will lead to your stories reaching your target audience more often and with more impact.

« Case Study »

But first I'd like to discuss how to "Google+" like a boss by sharing a case study from the Food Blogging industry: specifically, the meteoric rise of

Chef Dennis Littley. By Chef Dennis's own admission, food blogging is not, or, at least, was not a huge community on Google+ when he first arrived. Nor was Chef Dennis's blog audience the largest online.

But this didn't stop Chef Dennis from using Google+ to grow his follower base to over 665,000 people. Yes, a Food Blogging Chef without a TV show has over 665,000 followers on Google+ (and I know numbers don't mean everything, but it's an impressive accomplishment considering I know for fact he's done it completely white hat).

Chef Dennis does Google+ like a boss.

How did he do it?

He connected with established influencers in both the food blogging industry and Google+ community by providing them a platform to share their knowledge and expertise with his audience via Google Hangouts on Air. In the early days of Google+ Chef Dennis harnessed a tool most content marketers shied away from because of its newness. For most of 2013 and into 2014, Chef Dennis was one of the only chefs in the entire world connecting with his audience via Google Hangout on Air. Chef Dennis used Google+ and one of its most powerful and unique social features (Hangouts on Air) to become a leader within his industry.

After building up enough connections with influencers both inside and outside the food blogging industry throughout Google+, Chef Dennis became a creator, hosting the First Annual Google+ Bloggers Conference over the course of three days via Google Hangouts on Air, with topics ranging from SEO to content marketing to social media, podcasting and yes, even food blogging.

With the Google+ Bloggers Conference, Chef Dennis brought together all the essential elements to using **Google Plus like a Boss: Connect, Influence, and Create.**

To effectively grow your Google+ presence you MUST, to some degree, embody all three elements. For each of us, the mix will vary, but the essential elements remain the same.

» The Connector

The Connector knows everyone. A great example of this is Martin Shervington, the founder of *Plus Your Business* and Content Warfare Podcast guest. The Connector spends a large portion of their time on Google+ introducing like-minded individuals to one another. The Connector is more apt to scroll through their various circles in search of great posts to comment on, tagging any relevant thought-leaders to add their expertise and voice to the discussion. Ultimately, they build new connections and relationships where none may have existed before.

The Connector's value to the greater Google+ is their ability to bring separate yet related communities of people together helping to grow conversations and, in turn, their own presence on Google+, like a boss.

» The Influencer

The Influencer is the niche expert. Think Ronnie Bincer, founder of The Hangout Helper and Content Warfare Podcast guest. The Influencer spends the majority of their time educating and/or helping fellow members of the Google+ community. The Influencer builds communities dedicated to their area of expertise and is constantly searching Google+ through hashtags for conversations on their area of expertise all in an effort to provide more value.

The Influencer's value to Google+ is the knowledge and experience they can provide on a given topic. As their influence grows on a topic so does their following on Google+, like a boss.

» The Creator

The Creator is a little different. Think Demian Farnworth, Chief Content Officer at Copyblogger Media and Content Warfare Podcast guest. The Creator doesn't necessarily know everyone, nor are they an expert on any one topic. The Creator starts conversations through the sharing of images, articles, videos, quotes and thoughts that inspire discussion. The Creator is apt to be part of many communities, though may not manage or own any, and will build many unique, smaller circles for each one of their interests.

The Creator's value to Google+ lies in their ability to consistently share relevant, thought–provoking content with their community and inspire conversation. As the conversations grow, so does The Creator's following on Google+, like a boss.

» Like a Boss

When it comes to Google+, we all have different goals, different levels of success we're looking to attain. Regardless of what we're looking to achieve, success will come from embodying some mix of each The Connector, The Influencer and The Creator.

The mix is up to you, like a boss.

» How to Create Original Content on Google+

Once you understand the mix of personalities that drive success on Google+ (and in truth, these personalities transcend Google+ to pretty much all social settings), it's time to start creating original content.

Remember, creating original content inside of social media platforms can be dangerous business. But here's the rub: original content works on Google+. The Google+ community eats it up, and for good reason: original content takes thought, effort and time to create. But this deeper connection is exactly what an engagement–heavy social platform like Google+ wants.

If you're buying what I'm selling and want to start creating original content on Google+, here are seven simple tricks to create more engagement with original content on Google+.

1. Write a great headline.

A great headline is just as important for your Google+ posts as it is for your blog posts and YouTube videos. Make sure you wrap the headline in asterisks, *Headline Title*, to bold the lettering and attract more eyeballs.

2. Go long with your original Google+ content.

Think 350 – 750 words. The Google+ community wants meaty, thoughtful posts that force them to stop and think. These longer articles can often lead to more comments and re-shares from your audience. Again, the same concepts that apply to creating great content on your blog work on Google+. Deep, thought-provoking content that provides value to your audience is worth sharing. The opposite? Shallow link-dumps of articles serving as attempts at Google+ posts, but are really just lame efforts at getting website click-throughs.

If there is one activity that Google+ users in particular do not appreciate it is link-dumping. If you don't give Google+ users a reason to connect with you (i.e., valuable original content), they won't—and Google+ won't work to grow your audience or your business.

3. @mention relevant parties.

First, this is just good content marketing etiquette. Give credit where credit is due. Second, an @mention draws in the referenced party to potentially engage and share your content. So what does this look like?

Say I read an incredibly thought-provoking post on Fast Company's website, and would like to add my own thoughts and experiences to the discussion. In this case, I would share the Fast Company article on Google+. Then, in the body of the Google+ post, I would add my own original content.

This is where it's both proper etiquette and a good relationship-building strategy to @mention both Fast Company and the individual author of the original post. Additionally, if I'm including any thoughts from previous separate conversations on the topic, I may @mention those individuals or brands so they can weigh in on the topic as well. Drawing these relevant parties into the discussion creates a dynamic new discussions and potentially new relationships.

Do not—I repeat Do Not—just @mention 50 people with large followings on Google+ in the hopes they'll share your article. There are no situations where this is appropriate. If abused, this tactic is a quick way to get un-followed and/or blocked.

4. Link out to other posts/resources that support your

159

article.

Don't try to hog all the click-throughs for your own links. If you mention an article or a study or some other resource, link to it. Your original content is supposed to be valuable to the people reading it. Attribution is your friend. Linking out to other resources shows command and confidence for your area of expertise.

A great example of this is David Amerland and his "Sunday Read." If you are going to take original content on Google+ seriously, look up David (he's not hard to find on Google+) and study what he does in his weekly Sunday article.

Though the thoughts are always his own, every piece of reference material, whether it's his or not, is linked to. This creates a strong sense of trust between David and his audience. Readers know David is not creating this piece of content just for website traffic, but rather to add value to the lives of his audience.

160   **5.** Rich Media Rules

One of the most under-appreciated aspects of Google+ by marketers and business owners who aren't yet using the platform is its rich media-sharing capability. By rich media, we're talking about videos, gifs, audio and high-resolution images of almost every size and shape. Google+ is truly a rich media creators' paradise, and this is one of the qualities I'm most attracted to as a content marketer.

From within Google+, creators can share HD-quality YouTube videos, and have their audience watch from within a Google+ post. Gifs, moving images which people either love or hate (I happen to love), work a great change-up to still images found throughout most social networks. Podcasters share podcast episodes into Google+, and their audiences can listen from within Google+ posts.

Last, but certainly not least, Google+ allows high-resolution photos as large as 1200px tall by 800px wide. This provides the visual content marketer with a robust opportunity to capture attention with original content as Google+ users are scrolling down their Google+ streams.

6. Use an original content optin circle.

Circles are Google+'s method for segmenting connections within the platform. Though most social media networks have some format for segmenting connections, Google+ is unique in that circles are built into the framework of the platform and allow you to ping or notify connections within a circle(s) that a new piece of content has been published. Additionally, circles allow you to segment the content that enters your Google+ stream. You can create as many circles as you can dream up ways to segment your connections.

Because circles allow you to notify your connections of a new piece of content, they can act as a catalyst for attracting attention to specific post. However, with great power comes great responsibility. For, just as notifying a circle can increase engagement, spamming your connections with irrelevant content they're not interested is a good way to lose audience members.

The solution is to create an optin-circle. The process is pretty simple: every time you post a new piece of content on a given topic, at the bottom of the post ask interested parties to simply comment if they're interested in being notified of future posts on that given topic. Create a circle containing these individuals, and make sure to notify them each time you hit publish. By getting your connections' permission to notify them, you're building more trust with your audience more-momentum for your content.

161

7. Share out to other social networks.

Another unique and incredibly powerful feature of Google+ posts is that they are technically their own webpage. Click on the timestamp link in a Google+ post and you will be taken to the actual web page which contains your post. Then use a tool like BufferApp or Hootsuite to share that post out to Twitter, Facebook and LinkedIn. I've also found that sharing original Google+ posts that contain intriguing images on Pinterest increases overall engagement on that post.

This is another tactic you don't want to abuse, as some Google+ posts will not make sense to share on other social networks. Used sparingly, where appropriate, this tactic can drastically increase the attention your original Google+ posts receive.

→ The Rub

The point is, original content works on Google+. These seven tactics were tested and proved through my own work growing an audience on Google+. If you dive into creating original content that supports your overall brand message on Google+, you'll find even more tactics and strategies to expand reach and grow your own audience—not to mention your authority inside the Google universe.

The Devaluation of Unremarkable Content

The Internet is rapidly filling up with crappy, generic content.

Every day 2.73 million blog articles are published to the web. Many marketing experts, including many I love, would tell you that attention is not a zero sum game. There is truth to that . . . but it's damn close.

Let me quickly explain. There are only ten positions in organic search. Facebook only shows your content to somewhere around 6 – 16 percent of your fans. Tweets last only about 19 seconds before they're pushed out of view forever.

True, there is no finite limit on attention. I could give my attention to 1,000 articles, or to ten. And the pool of attention online only grows, as more people are drawn to the web, away from traditional media.

So what's the problem?

Attention is fleeting in nature, and discriminating in quality. Consumer attention will no longer tolerate unremarkable content.

I used to believe beginner bloggers needed to create more content, that traction came from activity. Like a rocket ship grasping for orbit, escape velocity was achieved through more publishing.

The thought was that early content would suck, and we needed to work through that phase in order to ever create valuable content. Over time, we'd find our voices, quality would increase, and hockey stick growth (rapid growth which when plotted on a chart looks like a hockey stick) would occur.

My mind has changed.

Quantity of content created is irrelevant to success.

You can post every day, or you can post once a month. It doesn't matter. Content saturation has devalued unremarkable content. Mark Schaefer, author, speaker and marketing consultant, wrote an epic and now main street blog post on this topic titled "Content Shock." The idea was that as more content is created every day, it becomes impossible to stand out, and our content marketing efforts produce a lower and lower ROI as content becomes a commodity.

This hypothesis isn't wrong. Average content is a commodity. There is way too much average content, and it looks and feels exactly the same. You know the type of content I'm talking about: unenthusiastic, uninspired, with little to no educational or entertainment value.

Content marketing works. . . it's just work.

It's true, your list post of seven generic reasons why something happens may receive more shares than a thought-provoking life experience story that exposes the root of a core issue your business solves. But which post type attracts more valuable attention? **Which type of post attracts the True Fans that will grow your business?**

Growing your audience of True Fans is the key. Web traffic and social sharing results are only supplemental indicators of attention. Comments display a deeper level of attention. Links back to your article from other blogs show even more attention. And what is in my opinion the most important indicator of attention, personal notes and emails.

Our goal in creating content, in sharing our ideas with the world, is not blog traffic. Our goal is to find believers. Our goal is to find True Fans. How many people took the time to send you an email or personal message on social media about your last list post?

None.

When's the last time you gave someone private props for a list post?

Never.

Because list posts (and other forms of half-hearted content creation) are unremarkable content. Not that you shouldn't create list posts. There is value in creating lists to supplement an overall content strategy (11 tools for this, 17 resources for that, etc.)—this type of content has its place. From a web traffic perspective, these gimmicky posts may even drive decent traffic. Just don't expect them to move the attention needle.

» What Remarkable May Be

"Remarkable" is a very esoteric idea. It's difficult to quantify "remarkable." It's difficult to build process and policy around "remarkable." "Remarkable" to me and my audience may not necessarily be "remarkable" to you and your audience. That's why nowhere in this book do I tell you exactly what to create.

I am not so arrogant, nor are you so naive, for either us to believe that in the pages of any book could be the exact solution to your unique content marketing strategy.

Your audience, your True Fans, are yours. **Only you know what "remarkable" content looks like in your world, and you must find your remarkable content.**

Your "remarkable" may be sharing your simple truth every day, like Seth Godin. Your "remarkable" may be videotaping yourself jumping out of a spaceship like Redbull. Your "remarkable" may be publishing a work which changes the public perception of what "career" means, like Tim Ferriss in The 4-Hour Work Week. Your "remarkable" may be supporting and mentoring someone without expectation of reciprocation, like Marcus Sheridan has done for me.

165

What makes you and your content remarkable will be unique. It will be yours and yours alone. It will separate you and define you. Your "remarkable" will attract the valuable, sticky attention your business needs to survive in today's content-saturated Internet.

Mark Schaefer was right: average, unremarkable content is a commodity and, in creating such content, your message (and your business) will never stand out. Your unremarkable content will look just like your competition's and be swept away in a content feed tidal wave, another drop in the Internet ocean, indistinguishable, unrecognizable and unimportant.

→ The Rub

Think of truly remarkable content (content that educates, entertains and inspires your True Fans) as a lighthouse standing tall at the edge of the rocks, wave upon wave crashing down, yet still the lighthouse shines for all to see. An unmistakable beacon of value in a sea of commodity.

To overcome the devaluation of unremarkable content, we must shift our focus from quantity (more or less) to high value: authentic pieces of content which educate, entertain and inspire our audience.

Do that–

Tap that vein–

. . . and your business will never want for attention again.

How To Keep Them Coming Back

What do we do once we have our audience's attention? How do we keep them coming back? How do we notify our audience that we've posted new content they will enjoy?

Let's start with how we notify them. There are two real schools of thought on this topic:

You choose a medium for communication, say email, which is the favorite of most Internet marketers. If someone enjoys your content and wants to be notified of updates, they must subscribe via email. We force the medium on them.

The second school of thought is the more democratic method, where we provide an assortment of options and allow our audience to choose the medium of notification they prefer.

I've struggled with this question for quite some time, going back and forth based on the latest convincing article I've read from someone experiencing success.

167

Take Derek Halpern, the founder of SocialTriggers.com. Derek would tell you that offering any option other than email for subscription is a waste of time and resources. There is no greater method than email for getting a group of people to take one single action in a given period of time. So why would we waste our time collecting subscribers in an RSS service or social media network? We want to own their email addresses, or at least the right to send them emails directly. That's how we get our products and services in front of them. That's how we make money online: we capture their email address and then send them offers.

Then we have Pat Flynn, founder of SmartPassiveIncome.com. Pat is famous for (and from) presentations on his "Be Everywhere" theory of marketing. Pat would tell you that, in order to attract the maximum audience, we must spread our message throughout the Internet in as many places as we can, using as many different mediums as we can. This can be an incredibly powerful strategy, but also very time consuming.

Both strategies are great, but limiting if you follow them as gospel. Here's the deal: Derek Halpern can force his audience to only subscribe by email because he's Derek Halpern, a no-excuses New Yorker who has provided incredible value, over and over again, for years. He is also connected to all of the biggest names and brands in the online marketing world. What I'm saying is he's earned the attention of enough people to allow him to say, "You subscribe by email, or you don't subscribe at all." If you put in the work that Derek has, this may be a completely viable strategy for your business.

Derek is also willing to work with a smaller than maximum audience because he knows, if you're willing to follow his rules, then you're also deeply invested in him as a content creator and value-provider. He's weeding out unqualified leads.

No one in business enjoys spinning their wheels, handling prospects who are unqualified or, even worse, clients that should have never become clients in the first place because they don't believe in you or your message.

168

In theory, I love the Pat Flynn "Be Everywhere" philosophy, but as I've dug deep into online marketing and online business building, it's become abundantly clear, over and over and over again, that:

1. We can't be everywhere, at least not at first.

2. Your audience doesn't necessarily want to see you everywhere, just where you do the best work.

A big part of finding success and growing your business online centers around number two.

Where do you do your best work? Where do you feel the most comfortable creating and distributing your message? It may be blogging or Instagram, or YouTube video. The medium itself is less important than your ability to create value there. If you suck at Twitter, why are you wasting valuable time and energy trying to build an audience on Twitter?

Here's how you figure out where you do your best

work. It starts by making three lists:

1. What do I enjoy creating about the most? This answer is going to include your passions, your interests, your hobbies.

At some point–and the timetable is different for everyone–content marketing becomes work. As we've discussed, this is a grinder's game. It helps if you're passionate about the topic you're creating content around.

The natural comment is, "Ryan, I need to create content on my business so that I can make money. That's why I bought your stupid book." Undoubtedly, your passions, interests and hobbies filter into your business, and/or the culture of the business you work for. List the topics where this happens.

2. What does your audience enjoy reading the most? This can be a little tricky because you're going to want to do some research. You may not currently be creating content around the topics that your audience most enjoys. Find out where your True Fans are hanging out online and take note of what gets the most interest.

3. What topics drive revenue to your business? This can even be drilled down to specific products and services inside your business. What products or services have the highest margins? What products or services drive the most revenue? For many businesses, the products and services with the highest margins may not drive the most revenue.

Now take these three lists and line them up.

Where do you see congruency? What topics are you passionate about, that your audience enjoys, that also are potential revenue-creating topics for your business?

Some of the connections will be direct. For an insurance agent, writing about golf makes complete sense. Golf is a favorite sport among business professionals, and a topic they'd most likely be interested in reading more about. Business insurance is a high-margin product for insurance agents, a product almost any insurance agent would love to sell more of.

So how does an insurance agent get her audience to keep coming back to her website? Write a weekly local golf course review, breaking down each hole. Add images and video to each post. She could even interview the course pro for a few "Insider" tips on how to score well at that particular course. Additionally, this insurance agent could share stories and lessons learned on the golf course, and how they apply to her business.

Golf course reviews aren't the only content on this insurance agent's website, but this is the content that keeps her audience coming back. Then, when her audience has an insurance issue, all they need to do is click around her site to find answers from the great insurance content she's already created. Buying insurance from her is the next natural step.

« The Content Warfare Case Study »

On June 8th of 2014, I launched the pre-order campaign for my first book: this book, *Content Warfare*, on a start-up crowdfunding platform, Publishizer. It's possible you are a contributor, an investor in *Content Warfare*, and thus played an enormous part in the birth of what you're reading right now.

My goal for the pre-order campaign was to raise $10,000 to pay for the expenses of producing the most professional self-published hardcover book possible. Twenty-one days later, my book project hit the $10,000 goal, breaking the previous funding record on Publishizer by two days.

This is called "Audience Activation," and it's key to how I successfully crowdfunded the *Content Warfare* book. The process of audience activation is how we ultimately extract value from the audience we've spent time building through all the methods and concepts explained in this book. The funding of *Content Warfare* is a case study in itself for the concepts contained within it. How meta is that?

171

As we walk through exactly how I was able to raise over $10,000 in 21 days to publish this book, in your mind replace 'crowdfunding a book' with your own content marketing goals. Everything we've learned in this book is played out in this case study, interchangeable with whatever the work is that you do.

» Responsibility

Why was a professionally published hardcover book important? Why would I spend the time, effort and money to professionally self-publish a hardcover book when throwing together an eBook of blog posts and uploading to Amazon may sell the same number of copies?

The answer is simple: I feel responsible to the *Content Warriors* who show up, day in and day out, to support my work.

Responsibility. That may seem like a strange word to use, especially in today's efficiency driven marketplace.

The *Content Warfare* Book is really a distillation of more than two years of conversations I've had on the *Content Warfare* Podcast with both the amazing guests who've taken their time to share expertise with us, and the amazing Content Warriors who continue to invest their time in the show.

More than two years (107 episodes as I'm writing this) of interviewing the Internet's most prolific content creators and extracting their secrets to winning the battle for attention online inspired this.

My audience deserves more than a thrown-together eBook. They deserve something tangible, something they can hold in their hands and be proud of, like I am when I re-read my physical copy of Gary Vaynerchuk's *Crush It* for the 17th time (That book still gets me jacked up every time I read it).

Creators have a responsibility to their audiences.

Creators have a responsibility to be authentic, transparent and honest in their work, to constantly push themselves to do better work, and to consider the value of every piece of content produced. The minute we lose that sense of responsibility, we lose our audience.

172

The hardcover copy of *Content Warfare* is my way of saying "thank you." Thank you for sticking with me. Thank you for investing yourself in me. Thank you for trusting me, for believing in me. Thank you for being a part of my life. **Thank you.**

» Crowdfunding and Self-Publishing

When I first decided to use a crowdfunding platform to self-publish *Content Warfare,* the idea was met with a bit of pushback and criticism.

"Isn't crowdfunding just a money grab?"

"If your idea is so great, why not just pay the upfront costs yourself?"

"If your book is worth publishing, why not use a traditional publisher?"

All valid questions worth responding to.

» Self-Publishing

The idea that somehow a self-published book is intrinsically a lesser quality product, solely because it's self-published, is preposterous. The work of authors like James Altucher (*Choose Yourself*) and Kamal Ravikant, (*Love Yourself Like Your Life Depends on It*) have completely destroyed this notion.

If you'd like an even deeper dive into self-publishing, visit http://www.ryanhanley.com/show84, and listen to the fantastic Joanna Penn, the bestselling self-published author, explain why. "Writing is for you," she says. "Publishing is for your reader."

As obvious a statement as this may seem, self-published books are only as good as the authors (and teams of professionals supporting those authors) who write them. In this way, self-published books are no different than any traditionally published book.

Apply this philosophy to your own content marketing efforts. True, you're not a traditionally-trained, seasoned media veteran, but that doesn't mean you don't have the ability to create immense value in your "self-published" work (i.e., blog posts, videos, podcasts, etc.).

173

Content marketing works . . . it's just work. You must hold yourself to the higher standard your audience deserves.

» Crowdfunding

Definition: Crowdfunding is the collection of finance from backers—the "crowd"—to fund an initiative.

It's really that simple. It's not a money grab. It's not a cop-out. Crowdfunding is an incredibly difficult and time-consuming process by which projects (like this book) are validated and audiences are activated.

This is what Natalie Sisson did when she crowdfunded her first book, *The Suitcase Entrepreneur*, and it became an Amazon #1 bestseller.

Crowdfunding doesn't limit upfront risk, it exposes opportunity. Learning from Natalie's example, I knew that successfully crowdfunding *Content Warfare* would mean two things:

1. The idea and concepts within the book had legs.

2. There was an audience for the book willing to spend money.

This is why we crowdfund a project, not just to raise money (though money is important), but to validate the idea and activate the audience that potentially resonates with the idea.

The same concepts apply in our content marketing efforts. The reason we build an audience *before* asking for the sale is to make sure that consumers exist that would be excited by (and willing to pay for) the product we sell.

This is why we ask our audience to connect with us on social media, or to opt-in to our email list or give us their contact information to sign-up for a webinar before we ask for the sale. We're validating the concept before asking for the sale.

» How to Activate Your Audience

It became very clear while crowdfunding *Content Warfare* that the process for success ran parallel to the principles we've learned throughout this book:

1. Build the audience.

2. Activate the audience.

3. Empower the audience.

There are tons of tactics and tricks for crowdfunding, but all of them fall under one of these three steps.

1. Build the Audience

You must build an audience of True Fans, (even a small audience), before you can expect anyone to support your crowdfunding project. There are many reasons that a crowdfunding campaign can fail, but from my experience, the number one reason is lack of audience. Where have we heard this before?

« ACTIVITIES »

Here are a few activities to build an audience prior to your crowdfunding campaign launch:

A. Start building a dedicated list (I did this with my *Content Warfare* Book Founding Members). Give these individuals bonuses on top of what everyone else has access to in exchange for their early commitment to your cause. In this case, "Founding Members," got to play an integral role in choosing the cover of this book, among other directional decisions. These people were supporters of *Content Warfare* at the deepest level.

Not all of these people contributed to the crowdfunding campaign, and that's OK. Letting people behind the curtain builds trust and appreciation. Never forget that content marketing is a long-game.   175

B. Create a private Google+ community or Facebook group dedicated to topics relevant to your project. These private communities and groups become your message board, a place for conversations to happen around topics your audience is interested in.

C. Drip teaser content (I did this with quotes from the book on Instagram that I then shared on Facebook and Google+) to attract people to your campaign. This is a practice that I carried throughout writing the entire book. It's easy to hibernate while working on a larger project. Dripping out small messages supporting your overall larger work helps to keep your project on your audience's mind.

It goes without saying that you must do these things with good intentions. Value to the audience is paramount. If you use these tactics to simply back your audience into a corner and then hard sell them, results will be limited.

2. Activate the Audience

Once you've built an audience that trusts you and is anticipating the start of your crowdfunding campaign, you're now ready to launch. The success or failure of your crowdfunding campaign will come out of your ability to drive your pre-existing audience to the campaign, not random people who find your campaign page. I'm an absolute believer in serendipity, but the customers who find you and your work through seemingly random ways are gravy, not the main course.

« ACTIVITIES »

Here are a few activities to activate your audience once your crowdfunding campaign has launched:

A. Send them emails announcing the launch.

There is no better way to get a group of people to take a single action in a given period of time than email. Believe that. Once you've built an audience, it's time to tell your story and explain how your audience can participate.

176

B. Send personal, one-to-one messages to influencers within your audience.

This can be done by email, phone, text or social media. The medium is less important than the personalized nature of the communication. We use digital tools to create human relationships. One-to-one messages may not scale, depending on the size of your project. However, building the right relationships with influencers who've spent time building an audience based on trust and respect (like you) can go a long way.

C. Post announcements of the campaign start in the private groups you've created.

Obvious, but important: these are the people most invested in the success of your work. Give them easy ways to share your campaign. I did this through tools like Click to Tweet and the aforementioned quote graphics.

Activating your audience is simply pointing them in a direction. If you've spent the time to build trust and respect, then activating your audience will not seem like a sales pitch, but just the next logical step in the relationship.

In the 100 Questions Answered Campaign, answering the questions was my attempt to build an audience around the boring topic of insurance. For the insurance consumers who followed along (or found the work sometime later), the next logical step in solving their insurance problems would be to pick up the phone and call our agency.

3. Empower the Audience

Any growth hacker worth his salt knows, once your audience has contributed to your campaign, the work has really just begun. It's imperative you provide contributors (customers, clients, etc.) with ways to share your campaign with their own audiences. This is how your campaign goes viral. It's the frosting on your crowdfunding cake.

Here are a few activities to empower your audience to share your crowdfunding campaign:

A. Use Click to Tweet links on your campaign page to share powerful quotes, ideas, and benefits from your project. Make it easy for your audience to share your project. Keep the barrier to sharing as low as possible. This increases the chance your audience will share your project with their own audiences.

177

B. Create images your audience will want to share in their social media networks. As I've mentioned before, throughout the entire process of writing *Content Warfare*, I've pulled out and shared what I felt were intriguing quotes made into graphics. (Primarily, I've used the smartphone app WordSwag, and the website Canva.com to create these graphics).

C. Create an intro/trailer video on YouTube for your project, explaining why people should care and contribute. By using YouTube for this video, you give your audience an easy-to-share format for the content. Make sure the video contains a call-to-action for your project. Landing pages with video convert at two to three times the rate of landing pages that don't. Video helps create the deeper emotional connection needed to get some audience members to crack their wallets.

D. Create a Slideshare document relevant to your project which contains quotes: how-to info or, if your project is a book, an excerpt broken out in a visually appealing way.

Make these shareable items valuable in their own right, and worthwhile for your audience to share. If these pieces are just billboards for your project, no one is going to care.

With each piece of collateral that I created for the *Content Warfare* book, I wanted my audience to think, "Geez, if a video or quote has this much value, then the book must be packed with great stuff."

This made a contribution to the book campaign a desired and logical next step.

→ The Rub

Crowdfunding is a nerve-racking and stressful process. But, done right, it can jumpstart the success of your project or product unlike any other launch process that exists.

It was humbling to receive the support I did for the *Content Warfare* book. It took me a long time to build the audience that made the *Content Warfare* crowdfunding campaign a success. They are a testament to the power of building an audience the right way–through trust and respect–before ever asking for a sale.

For when an audience trusts and respects you and/or your business, they don't buy from you just because they need what you sell. Rather, they feel like they are part of your success. That, my friends, is how you win in the battle for attention online.

I know this all sounds mad. I've written an entire book, spending countless hours attempting to convince you to *stop* trying to sell your product or service online.

Indulge me: let's take a trip down the rabbit hole.

No more sales pitches disguised as blog posts.
No more "Buy Now" social media posts.
No more pushy direct mail tactics.

We're bludgeoning consumers with our online sales message, and it's simply not working.

Our traffic isn't growing.
We're not capturing new leads.
No one is buying from us online.

The problem is simple: we're trying to sell online.

Truly gifted content marketers never sell; rather, they sell without selling. They sell because they do everything *but* sell. Please don't pass this off as naive blogger-speak, and then mumble something to yourself about Return on Investment as you close the book.

Think back to everything we've discussed, and consider who you're marketing to: the Connected Generation, people who digest information through smartphones, listen to podcasts while they work out and build blogs to share their own experiences with the world.

The Connected Generation doesn't need nor does it want you selling them anything. **The Connected Generation wants to feel the sense of empowerment that comes from choosing you.** Steve Martin famously said about show business, "Be so good they can't ignore you." In content marketing, you must "Be so good, they can't help but choose to business with you."

182 Which only happens when we forget about selling, and focus on educating, entertaining and inspiring our audience over and over and over again.

Direct mail sales tactics may still work on Unconnected Generation consumers who aren't current on the products and services available in the market. The Unconnected Generation must have their life interrupted with advertising to stay current on the marketplace.

But the Connected Generation has the tools, resources and, most importantly, the desire to research and stay up-to-date on the latest trends in the products and services they need. This is basically the defining principle of being a member of the Connected Generation (remember age, sex, creed, and race don't matter).

Connected Generation consumers live public lives, and the things they purchase are a direct representation of who they are. Every purchase is on display. We want to be able to tell our friends and our family what an amazing experience we had purchasing a product, and how awesome we are for having done so.

Connected Generation consumers use brands as form of self-expression. We, as Content Warriors, must create an experience and perception around our product or service that matches the type of consumer we wish to attract. This is our story.

If you've made it this far, then you must believe my mad notion that hard sales tactics and interruption marketing are not the answer.

I want you to forget about sales funnels, pay-per-click advertisements and long landing pages filled with bright yellow highlighted copy. These are tactics.

Instead, **focus on educating, entertaining and inspiring your audience.** If, in doing this, you need sales funnels, pay-per-click advertisements and long landing pages filled with bright yellow highlighted copy, so be it.

Don't sell to your audience; become part of your audience. Give without expectation of reciprocation. Be authentic, transparent and honest. Spill the Simon Sinek "Why" of your business out on the table, and the Connected Generation soak it up.

183

I'm not crazy.

I simply believe—and hope you do, too—the successful brands of our future will dedicate themselves to integrating into communities of people and deliver unyielding value before ever asking for a sale . . . or maybe we are mad.

Golf Lesson in Content Marketing Success

"Success in golf depends less on strength of body than upon strength of mind and character." ~ Arnold Palmer

As a Christmas present, my father-in-law gave me two golf lessons at a local country club. A lifetime of playing baseball has ruined any chance I may have had at a naturally successful golf swing and, honestly, I think he's sick of beating the pants off me. Two golf lessons were a much appreciated gift.

I had not met the golf pro before and, upon our introduction, I didn't have high hopes. His cordial half smile gave away that he was probably a pleasant man, but this was most certainly a business transaction. When we got to the range, I took five swings to get loosened up and give him a feel for what he was about to work with. As I stood over the ball for my sixth shot, I asked the Pro, "What should I be working on? What's a drill I should be doing at home to improve?"

184

His answer, as matter-of-fact as could be, has changed the way I view achievement and success. "How about you focus on where you want the ball to go, and then put it there?"

I was floored. What about mechanics? What about setup? What about positioning?

The golf pro continued, "Tiger Woods sees the game of golf differently than you do, and it has nothing to do with mechanics. Every shot, no matter if it's on the (driving) range, Augusta or mini-golf, Tiger Woods focuses on nothing else other than where he wants the ball to go and what he wants it to do when it gets there. He visualizes every aspect of the journey the ball will take to get to his desired destination. Then he swings. Forget about mechanics; your body knows what to do. The hard part for amateur golfers is focusing on what they actually want to happen."

When he finished speaking, I found myself staring at him, awkwardly. "The hard part for amateur golfers is focusing on what they actually want to happen."

Who was this guy? Was Arnold Palmer incognito, teaching golf in Upstate New York?

As it turns out, my golf pro is no one of overt distinction; he's a man who'd studied the game of golf for a long time. What he didn't realize is that he had not only given me the secret to a better golf game, but also content marketing success.

» The Goal Dictates the Mechanics

Over the course of producing the *Content Warfare* Podcast for over two years and 107 episodes, I've received hundreds of questions from listeners. These questions are one of my favorite parts of producing the show, a true testament to work and its impact. The vast majority of the time, these questions involve tactics. Unfortunately, tactics (mechanics) don't help us reach our goals *if we don't know what those goals are.*

This was the lesson of my golf instructor, and the message I've attempted to burn in your brain with this book. Focusing on tactics is like pushing a rope: all pain, no gain. Ours goals dictate the tactics we use. 185

→ The Rub

Here's how we harness this wisdom to achieve content marketing success:

1. Take out a piece of paper and write your most critical content marketing goal at the top as large as you can (i.e., capture new email subscribers).

2. Now quantify that goal (i.e., 1,000 new subscribers).

3. Below this, write a one-sentence description of why this is your most important goal (for example, "With 1,000 new subscribers, I can extract enough new clients to start my own business.")

4. Next, write down the timeframe in which you need this to happen (i.e., "For my own sanity, I need this happen in six months.")

5. Finally, visualize the path to capturing new email subscribers and write a list, in order of importance, the tactics that will help you achieve your goal (i.e., create free eBook, build landing page, find relevant blogs for guest post opportunities, etc.).

When you reach Step Number 5, it's OK to start thinking about tactics. If your goal is to grow your audience, then the tactics could potentially include email list-building and increasing your connection on Google+ . If your goal is to grow your business revenue, then the tactics could potentially be completely different depending on timeframe and target audience.

Goal dictates tactic.

So the question becomes:

→ What is your goal?

Yesterday's Homerun

"Yesterday's home runs don't win today's games." ~ Babe Ruth

There is a drive in certain individuals . . check that. It's not necessarily drive. It's not passion. It's not responsibility. It's not dedication or desire.

It's the uncomfortable chafing of satisfaction.

Certain individuals are just uncomfortable standing still, a trait that causes them to always push forward.

Babe Ruth set the all-time career home run record at 139 in 1921.

He then went on to hit another 575 home runs in his career for a total of 714. Think about that for a second. He was the all-time career home run leader. No one had ever hit as many home runs as Babe Ruth. His place in history was set, yet he pushed himself to hit another 575.

187

I'd like to think this constant push forward is forgetfulness, but it's not. We don't forget the achievements of yesterday, we celebrate them briefly, maybe, but ultimately these individuals are always unsatisfied.

The truth is, for all the personal issues Babe Ruth created for himself, he was utterly unsatisfied with yesterday's achievements.

We can learn from this.

It's not healthy to be so unsatisfied with your achievements, you let your life fall apart despite your success. That's where Babe Ruth made his mistakes, and paid for them.

What we learn is that being overly satisfied with yesterday, creates complacency today. Complacency today destroys success tomorrow.

» Permission to Start

"Successful people are not gifted; they just work hard, then succeed on purpose." ~ G.K. Nielson

It's time to get to work. You now own the core principles for winning the battle for attention online and should be pretty jacked up for the opportunity literally at your fingertips.

I hate the word "hustle," mostly because it's overused by marketers and personal brands who don't actually embody 'hustle.' The word has lost significance in the echo chamber of self-help gurus and marketing ninjas. But I love "hustle," the action. It's how we win at content marketing. We can't out-spend, we can't out-network and, in most cases, we can't out-talent our competition. To try is futile, because all these things are fleeting. No matter how much money you spend, who you know and how smart you think you are, eventually someone will come along with more money, more contacts and more brilliance.

It's the workers, the doers, the "hustlers" that win at the attention game. Anyone that tells you different is trying to sell you something that won't work in the long-game. The winners of *Content Warfare* have money plus hard work, contacts plus hard work, talent plus hard work: that's their secret.

Every person I've mentioned throughout the course of this book, both in-depth and in passing, has worked his or her ass off for every eyeball of attention enjoyed today. I hope if you've taken anything away from this book it's that chasing tactics and strategies is not the path to success. There are basic principles of building human relationships and distributing your message which attract revenue-producing attention; the tactics and strategies are born out of your work.

"Good things may come to those who wait, but only the things left by those who hustle." - Inaccurately attributed to Abraham Lincoln (but perfect)

As far back as I can remember I've always been attracted to the possibility of inspiration.

As I child, I would have had no way of expressing this understanding. Only as an adult have I been able to verbalize the feeling, the desire, I have to surround myself with **Inspiration.**

Whether it's a moment of self-realization or shared personal connection exchanged with an event attendee after a presentation, that lightning bolt of electric inspiration is intoxicating. My muse, the pool from which climbs my creativity.

But inspiring moments are fleeting. If we wait for inspiration to do our creative work, the work will never get done. We must be more tactical about our content marketing activities in order to push through the periods of time when our inspiration bucket is empty.

To win at Content Warfare, to ensure that we always have a story to tell, we must be open to inspiration in seemingly mundane activities.

This may sound like philosophical bullshit. You're an adult (most likely) and you don't need some guy from Upstate NY telling you how to live your life. What the hell do I know, right?

First, I love your questioning nature. You're making it hard for me to crack your egg, and I dig that.

Here's what I know: I know "The Grind." I know waking up every morning to the same dead-end job, dreading the commute, but even worse than that, dreading having to talk myself out of jacking my car into the next bridge abutment instead of putting up with one more day of pushing papers around my desk.

Before I began working at my insurance agency, before content marketing, I worked for two different Fortune 500 companies, one in accounting and one in finance. Not because of any fault of two these companies, I hated every second. Being a junior analyst for anyone pretty much sucks. Every day I went to work with the feeling that I didn't control my own destiny.

I lived in a constant state of being uninspired.

Inspiration is a fickle lover. You make yourself available or she moves on. This was a lesson I hadn't learnt yet at these first two jobs.

As much as I never had any intention of ever working in the insurance industry, my position as an insurance producer was the hard slap across the face that I needed to wake up and realize that the only person in charge of my destiny was me.

This is what telling your story allows you to do: take control of your destiny. When you tell your story online over and over again, you fix the game in your favor. You're letting the world know exactly what you want it to do. Before I found content marketing, before I had a medium with which to tell my story, it always felt like someone else was in control of the message.

But when we become creators, when we open our minds to the possibility of inspiration, tell the world exactly what we want out of it and seize the opportunities that present themselves, we begin to become better versions of ourselves.

190

"People think that stories are shaped by people. In fact it's the other way around." ~ Terry Pratchett, novelist

You're going to have days that seem void of creativity and originality. Become comfortable with this fact of content marketing. There's no tool, trick, tip, tactic or strategy that will allow you to sidestep "The Block," and "The Block" does not discriminate. Yet professional content marketers continue to create content at a relentless pace, where amateurs find themselves bloodied, beaten and licking their wounds as far from a keyboard as possible.

How do the professionals do it? The answer to this question is also the secret to creating more content. **The inevitability of "The Block" is not an excuse to stop creating.** This is what professional content marketers realize that everyone else does not. If we're going to successfully leverage the power of content marketing to attract attention, capture leads and make sales, we have to create more content, and we can't create more content by shutting down every time we don't feel original or inspired.

Every piece of content we create does not need to be Shakespeare. There are going to be days when every word will be clumsy and disconnected. Verbal vomit, if you will. Your thoughts will not be coherent, and your conclusions will miss the mark. Flat out, there will be days you suck at creating marketing.

But we must create through those days. If you can't squeeze an ounce of originality or personality or creativity out of your brain, then write whatever mundane, trivial thought is bouncing around in that cavernous cranium. We don't have to move mountains every day. We simply need to create every day. Content marketing is a grind. We know this.

If we write through the hard days, the easy days will be really easy.

Professional content marketers write because they have to, because it's who they are, because we never know when our Muse will decide to tap us on the shoulder and deliver our symphony. If we're not at the keyboard than our small moments of brilliance may never take a breath. Here's a truth I've learned from experience writing over 400 blog posts in 2012: the waves of creative genius have a way of favoring those who put in the work. You must put in the work to ride the waves.

191

Create till your fingers bleed, till scabs form, till your rough callused fingertips would make a banjo player jealous, then create more. Because it's here, when the pain of creation no longer exists, that our mind is truly free to see what needs to be said. The turn of phrase, the twist of tongue, the innuendo at just the right instant to entice your audience to take action.

Brilliance.

Just like life, creation is a gift. We must nurture and feed that gift, never taking for granted its fickle, delicate nature by assuming we can command creativity to respond at our whim.

Creating more content for your business or brand or mission has nothing to do with making time or coming up with new ideas. You simply have to write. Julia Cameron, author of *The Artist's Way*, calls this her "Morning Pages." Three full pages of writing every morning about anything and everything, whatever is on your brain at that moment. If the only thing you can think of is that you hate writing, then your three pages that morning will be filled with, "I hate writing" over and over. Embrace the failure and awfulness of your early writing efforts. If you're worried about sucking, then you probably do and that's completely okay. Everyone sucks when they start.

Tragic failure is never starting in the first place.

→ **Give yourself permission to start, today.**

Dare to Be First

"Screw it, let's do it." ~ Richard Branson

Every morning we start as just another entry in a horse race.

We saddle up, mount up and step into the gate.

Side by side we wait, the stink of nervous energy permeates the starting gate.

Waiting for the bell, expectation and a few rusty iron bars is all that separates us from the competition.

And then the silence hits...

...silence,

...silence,

The world is still moving, the crowd is still cheering, but our world is silent. This is the deafening quiet of anticipation meeting expectation. Then...

Bang!

Growing up 30 minutes from Saratoga Race Course, "The Track" is part of who I am. It's in my blood.

At 32 years old, I still get just as giddy on the quick drive up the Northway as I did when I was a child. I've witnessed hundreds of horse races over the years.

Every new race excites my soul.

People who don't frequent The Track, don't understand. They think it's about gambling (or worse, about winning money. Ha!)

For me, The Track has nothing to do with gambling, and horses are only part of it.

Ryan Hanley

The beauty in horse racing is recognizing the moment when a horse decides to finish first.

Yes, decides. I know the jockey plays a role in every run, but the jockey's job is really just to put the horse in position. The horse has to decide to finish first.

This moment is the electricity of life in its purest form.

The ears pin back.

The head pushes down.

The horses's gait changes.

The path becomes determined.

That horse, whether maiden or Grade I veteran, has decided to be first on this day.

It's amazing.

Some horses have this ability. The desire to finish first lives deep within them, passed along some bloodline. When the moment is right, they're able to call upon that desire.

Other horses don't. They just run. They run the race. With the right jockey, with the right conditions and right competition, they may even win.

For these horses, their victories, often small and infrequent, are not the result of will or determination, but rather a little bit of luck and a lot of circumstance.

In this capacity, I believe we humans differ from horses.

It's not in our bloodlines to finish first.

It's in our own minds. Each individual mind. Yours. Mine. Everyone.

We must dare to be first.

Dare to take the lead . . .

. . . to step forward

. . . to take charge.

Fate may decide the winner. That doesn't mean you need to let Fate's decision be an easy one.

I can't teach you to decide.

There are no tactics for deciding to finish first.

You must want it.

I can only make you aware of your ability. The rest is up to you.

Dare to be first.

Have the audacity to believe you are worthy.

Then, like the Thoroughbred you are:

→ Take Action!

I'm going to leave you with this great quote from Robert Ringer, author of *Action! Nothing Happens Until Something Moves*:

"I am absolutely convinced that neither success nor happiness is possible without action . . . Ideas can be precious commodities that can change the world. Sound preparation is invaluable, and knowledge and wisdom are essential when it comes to giving one an edge in the pursuit of great achievements.

195

"But ideas, preparation, knowledge and wisdom are all but useless without action because action is the starting point of all progress. In other words, an idea of and by itself has no intrinsic value. It must be accompanied by action. It is action that cuts the umbilical cord and brings an idea out of the womb."

The decision is yours, my friend. You now have the foundation for content marketing success. **It's time to find your audience, tell your story and win the battle for attention online.**

I'm out.

Ryan Hanley

"Grow your audience, grow your business."

» Author's Note: Continuing the Conversation

This book is my best effort at real magic. Not sleight of hand, or some extravagantly-orchestrated illusion like you might see on TV, but real magic. *Content Warfare* is the tangible manifestation of the principles of beliefs that guide me, not just as content marketer or business professional, but as a person.

Give without expectation of reciprocation.

I believe in the serendipitous nature of the world. I believe that, if we allow ourselves such hubris, practicing the lessons I've shared throughout the pages you've just read will help stack the deck in your favor. You will poke the Muse.

If you've decided to give in to the creative calling, if you believe that building an audience of True Fans is the only sustainable course to consistent business growth, then our conversation has only begun.

Connect with me on Google+ or send me an email **ryan@ryanhanley.com** if you'd like to chat in more detail about anything you read in the book.

#ContentWarfare

If you have questions, comments, or just want to rap about the concepts of Content Warfare, use the hashtag #contentwarfare on Google+, Twitter or Instagram. Take a photo of your Content Warfare book "In the Wild" and you could win a cool prize. Visit **contentwarfarebook.com** for details.

Content Warfare Live

Finally, if you think your company, customers or attendees at your next event would be inspired by the message within *Content Warfare*, please let me know. I love addressing corporate and conference audiences, showing them how to find their audiences, tell their stories, and win the battle for attention online.

I'd love to talk about the book, answer questions, or simply stay connected. Email me at **ryan@ryanhanley.com**.

» Notes / References

Godin, Seth - http://sethgodin.typepad.com/seths_blog/2014/04/trust-and-attention-the-endless-dance.html

Zero-sum game - http://en.wikipedia.org/wiki/Zero-sum_game

Attention Zero-sum game - http://abnormalreturns.com/attention-is-a-zero-sum-game/

From Attention to Engagement - http://www.learcenter.org/pdf/Barcelona2012.pdf

Attention Statistics: http://www.statisticbrain.com/attention-span-statistics/

Digital Attention Span - http://www.theguardian.com/media-network/media-network-blog/2012/mar/19/attention-span-internet-consumer

Brand Impressions: http://articles.latimes.com/2012/jul/08/business/fi-ct-digital-ads-20120708/2

Time Metrics - http://contently.com/strategist/2014/02/27/death-to-pageviews-all-hail-engaged-time-the-new-king-of-content-metrics/

Content Marketing Metrics 2013 - http://contently.com/strategist/2013/10/30/you-like-me-you-really-like-me-content-delivers-big-time-brand-lift/

Content Marketing Metrics 2014 - http://contently.com/strategist/2014/04/04/10-charts-that-are-changing-the-way-we-measure-content/

Pageviews Metrics - http://time.com/12933/what-you-think-you-know-about-the-web-is-wrong/

Content Marketing Facts - http://kapost.com/content-marketing-facts

Search Engine Watch - http://searchenginewatch.com/article/2340758/What-Type-of-Content-Should-You-Create-Long-or-Short

Argument Against Content Marketing - http://www.forbes.com/sites/mikalbelicove/2013/09/10/content-marketing-study-suggests-most-content-marketing-doesnt-work/

Why Does Content Go Viral - http://okdork.com/2014/04/21/why-content-goes-viral-what-analyzing-100-millions-articles-taught-us/

Audience Research - https://www.distilled.net/content-guide/

Sticky Traffic Data - https://blog.shareaholic.com/social-media-traffic-trends-04-2014/

Email Marketing Stats - http://hub.uberflip.com/h/i/9048279-infographic-10-stats-showing-that-email-marketing-is-more-alive-than-ever/15819

Inbound Marketing Trends 2014 - http://moz.com/blog/2014-inbound-marketing-trends

197

Video Marketing Stats - http://www.videobrewery.com/blog/18-video-marketing-statistics

Digital Attention - http://www.wired.com/magazine/2010/05/ff_nicholas_carr/

Psychology of Buying - http://www.psychologytoday.com/blog/inside-the-consumer-mind/201302/how-emotions-influence-what-we-buy

The Connected Consumer - http://www.slideshare.net/OgilvyAction/brand-connected-consumerresearch

New York Times Innovation Report - http://www.niemanlab.org/2014/05/the-leaked-new-york-times-innovation-report-is-one-of-the-key-documents-of-this-media-age/

Psychology of Belief - http://socialtriggers.com/gluten-sensitivity-myth/

Brand Self-Expression - http://www.brandeo.com/content/self-expressive-brands-building-brand-enabling-customer-self-expression

Brands Don't Connect - http://www.marketingcharts.com/wp/traditional/almost-half-of-us-consumers-emotionally-indifferent-to-brands-43121/ and http://www.marketingcharts.com/wp/traditional/only-1-in-10-consumers-feel-that-brands-are-doing-well-at-connecting-with-them-where-are-brands-failing-most-37199/

Content Marketing ROI - http://marketeer.kapost.com/wp-content/uploads/2012/06/Content-Marketing-Kapost-Eloqua-eBook.pdf

Psychology and UX Design - http://thehipperelement.com/post/87574750438/ux-crash-course-user-psychology

Blogging Survey Orbit Media - http://www.orbitmedia.com/blog/blogger-analysis/

Kelly, Kevin 1,000 True Fans - http://kk.org/thetechnium/2008/03/1000-true-fans/

MarketingProfs - http://www.marketingprofs.com/charts/2013/12095/b2b-buyers-prefer-short-content-and-rely-heavily-on-google-searches

Jasper Tourism Case Study - file:///Users/ryanhanley/Downloads/casestudytourismjasperv2july23-140731180859-phpapp02.pdf

Brogan, Chris - http://chrisbrogan.com/what-it-takes-to-be-an-overnight-success/

Long-Tail Keyword Conversion - http://searchenginewatch.com/article/2132155/On-Page-Optimization-Not-Dead-Long-Tail-Keywords-Increase-Rankings-Conversions-STUDY

Decline in Newspapers - http://www.slate.com/blogs/moneybox/2014/04/28/decline_of_newspapers_hits_a_milestone_print_revenue_is_lowest_since_1950.html

199

About the Author

Ryan Hanley loves good stories, cold beer, writing, the Buffalo Bills, horse racing, the *Content Warfare* Podcast, his wife Lauren and his son, The Duke. In reverse order . . . He's the President of Hanley Media Lab, a content marketing strategy firm helping brands grow their audience, to grow their business.

His *Content Warfare* Podcast (**www.contentwarfarepodcast.com**) has been consistently ranked as one of iTunes top content marketing podcasts for two years. You can find more of Ryan's writing on his content marketing blog (**www.ryanhanley.com**) as he dives deeper into the concepts and principles driving online business growth.

Connect with Ryan on Google+ (**google.com/+ryanmhanley**) and **@RyanHanley_com**.

Hanley Media Lab

Made in the USA
Las Vegas, NV
30 July 2021